THE VIRTUALLY
FAT-FREE
COOKBOOK

CLB 4898

© 1997 by CLB International, a division of Quadrillion Publishing Ltd

Printed and Bound in Italy by New Interlitho Italia S.P.A.

9 8 7 6 5 4 3 2 1
Digit on the right indicates the number of this printing

Library of Congress Cataloging-in-Publication Number 96-69250

ISBN 0-7624-0004-8

This book was designed and produced by CLB International
Godalming, Surrey, England, GU7 1XW

NUTRITIONAL CONSULTANCY by Jill Scott
PROJECT MANAGEMENT by Jo Richardson
PRODUCED by Anthology
ORIGINAL DESIGN CONCEPT by Roger Hyde
DESIGN MANAGEMENT by Rhoda Nottridge
PAGE MAKE-UP by Vanessa Good
PHOTOGRAPHY by Don Last; Sheila Terry — *jacket, pages 72-3*
HOME ECONOMY by Christine McFadden and Joy Parker
AMERICAN ADAPTATION by Josephine Bacon
PRODUCTION DIRECTOR: Gerald Hughes
PRODUCTION by Ruth Arthur, Karen Staff, Neil Randles, and Paul Randles

AUTHOR'S ACKNOWLEDGMENT
*I would like to thank Jo Richardson for inviting me to write this book,
and for her patience and good humor during the editing process. Many
thanks also to Katey Balfrey for her tireless testing of recipes, to Don Last
for the photography, and to Pat Bacon for the nutritional analysis.*

Published by Courage Books,
an imprint of Running Press Book Publishers
125 South Twenty-second Street
Philadelphia, Pennsylvania 19103-4399

THE VIRTUALLY
FAT-FREE
COOKBOOK

Christine McFadden

COURAGE
BOOKS
AN IMPRINT OF RUNNING PRESS
PHILADELPHIA • LONDON

CONTENTS

INTRODUCTION

*N*utritional recommendations seem to come and go as often as the seasons, but the one topic on which the experts all agree is the need to cut down drastically on the amount of fat in the diet. Only by doing so can we reduce the risk of succumbing to modern diseases such as coronary heart disease, stroke, and some cancers.

The problem with fat is that it makes food taste better and it leaves us feeling satisfied. So making a drastic and permanent reduction is no small feat. If you enjoy food and cooking, and if you want to cut out the fat but not the enjoyment, then this book is a must for you.

The Virtually Fat-Free Cookbook offers mouthwatering but virtually fat-free recipes for all tastes and occasions. All the recipes contain 5 grams (about 1 teaspoon) or less of fat per serving, and are based on sound nutritional principles. The book also contains easy-to-follow information about the relationship between food, nutrition, and health, based on the latest international scientific reports. It includes practical nutritional advice explaining the role of fat in the diet, how to reduce fat intake without compromising meal quality, and how to establish sensible eating patterns.

The Virtually Fat-Free Cookbook is aimed at anyone who enjoys food and cooking but who would like to dramatically reduce their fat consumption as part of a healthier eating and improved lifestyle program. It will also benefit those people who need to lose weight, or who need to minimize the fats in their diet for other reasons.

MAINTAINING BALANCE IN A VIRTUALLY FAT-FREE DIET

The nutrients in food do not work in isolation. They form a tightly knit team which supplies the body's entire needs. Fortunately, most foods are a complex mixture of several nutrients, so even if you have radically reduced your fat intake, you'll still be getting all the nutrients you need as long as you choose a variety of foods each day from the major food groups.

Imagine the food groups as a pyramid, with the types we need most forming the base, and the foods we need least at the top.

● CEREALS, POTATOES, RICE, BEANS, BREAD, AND PASTA
Eat as much as you like of these carbohydrate-rich, energy-producing foods. They form the base of the pyramid and should make up well over half of your daily diet. This is vital if you are following a virtually fat-free diet, since you'll need to replace the energy normally provided by fat.

● VEGETABLES AND FRUITS
These foods form the next level of the pyramid. Eat as many of them as you like — they're virtually fat-free and packed with fiber, minerals, and vitamins. Vegetables and fruits are an invaluable source of a particular group of vitamins (A, C, and E) known as antioxidants, which are believed to help prevent some cancers.

Leading health organizations recommend consuming at least five servings of different fruits and vegetables each day, excluding potatoes. For many people, this represents a 50% increase of current intakes.

● MEAT, FISH, POULTRY, AND EGGS
We need far less of these protein-rich foods than previously imagined. Red meat, oily fish, and egg yolk are high in fat. The most useful foods in this group are white-fleshed fish and skinless chicken or turkey, which can replace ground beef or lamb in many recipes. Egg yolks are high in fat but the whites contain very little, so substitute two or three whites for one egg when making egg-based dishes.

● MILK, YOGURT, AND CHEESE

Dairy foods are high in saturated fats and cholesterol, and should be restricted to the minutest amounts if you're following a very low-fat diet. Eaten in small quantities, they provide useful amounts of calcium and protein, and they also replace the flavor and moisture normally provided by fats and oils. There are reduced-fat and virtually fat-free versions of these foods, so there's no need to banish them completely.

● FATS, OILS, AND SUGARS

These concentrated, energy-rich foods form the tip of the pyramid, and are needed only in very small quantities. However, fats and oils should not be excluded completely since they play an essential role in a healthy balanced diet.

THE ROLE OF FAT

Although it is true that most of us should be careful about the amount of fat in our diet, this does not mean that fat should be avoided at all costs. We all need some fat. It is an important source of energy and essential nutrients, and it plays a vital role in bodily functions.

Weight for weight, fat provides about double the energy of carbohydrates. Therefore, only very small quantities need be eaten. It is an important nutrient for babies and for very young children who are growing rapidly.

The body stores excess fat and deposits some of it under the skin. This provides insulation and helps prevent heat loss when the body is exposed to very low temperatures.

Fats also contain the fat-soluble vitamins A, D, E, and K, as well as essential fatty acids.

Foods with a high fat content have a rich, satisfying flavor and, because we digest fat more slowly than other nutrients, they have what is known as a high satiety value. In simple terms, that means they leave us with a satisfying feeling of fullness which is hard to beat. Fats also act as a kind of culinary moisturizer — they improve the palatability of foods and make us want to eat more of them.

DIFFERENT TYPES OF FAT

All fats contain a mixture of fatty acids: saturated, monounsaturated, and polyunsaturated differ in chemical structure and, to some extent, in the functions they perform. If the proportion of saturated fatty acids is greater than polyunsaturated, the fat is said to be saturated and vice versa.

As a general rule, saturated fats are solid at room temperature and tend to come from animal sources, while polyunsaturated fats are usually liquid and are vegetable fats. The two exceptions are coconut oil and palm oil, both of which are rich in saturated fats.

Monounsaturated fats come from olive oil, canola oil, nuts, seeds, and meats.

A high intake of saturated fats is associated with raised blood cholesterol levels and the associated risk of heart disease. Recent studies have shown that monounsaturated fats can protect against heart disease by lowering blood cholesterol.

Polyunsaturated fats provide the body with the "essential" fatty acids, needed in small amounts to maintain good health. Even if you're on a very low-fat diet, you are probably getting enough as long as the fats you actually use are high in polyunsaturates. Vegetable oils such as sunflower, safflower, and soya are good sources.

DAILY FAT ALLOWANCE

The current nutritional advice is to limit daily fat intake to no more than 30-35% of total calories, with a lower limit of 15% for people at risk from heart disease. Experts recommend that less than 10% of energy requirements should come from saturated fatty acids. But what do these percentages mean in real terms? How much fat is 30% of calories?

If we take as an example a woman on a calorie-controlled diet of 1,200 calories a day, 30% of her energy intake would be 360 calories. Since each gram of fat provides 9 calories, 360 calories is 40 grams of fat.

In order to calculate your daily fat allowance, you need to establish your ideal weight, taking into account your height, build, age, level of activity, and overall health. If you want to lose weight, you might aim for a daily intake of 1,200 or 1,000 calories.

So how much is a gram of fat in terms of actual food servings? Probably more than you think. Just one tablespoon of French dressing contains 7 grams of fat, a boiled egg has 6 grams, and a handful of dry-roasted peanuts has 12 grams. It's easy to use up your fat allowance unless you make a point of becoming familiar with the fat content of a typical serving of food.

FAT-FREE STRATEGIES

Even if you have already reduced the fat in your diet to healthier levels, making a further reduction to under 5 grams of fat per serving does require that extra surge of willpower. Fortunately, there are strategies which will ensure that preparing, cooking, and eating food can still remain one of the greatest joys of life.

There are a surprising number of cooking techniques that don't require fat — simmering, dry-frying, broiling, microwaving, and pressure-cooking, to name a few. They also have the added benefit of not creating greasy dishes which need cleaning after the meal.

Flavor is an important element that people miss when they first give up fat. However, the richness of fat often masks more interesting and subtle flavors in the food. As your palate becomes clearer, you'll start to appreciate clean, natural tastes. If strong, satisfying flavors are what you enjoy, there is a wealth of aromatics and seasonings that offer exciting possibilities in place of fat — chilies, garlic, ginger, grated citrus rind and juice, soy sauce, pickles, wine, spirits, vegetable juices, sun-dried tomatoes, herbs, and spices will get your tastebuds tingling.

Fats also help to improve the appearance, palatability, and keeping qualities of food, particularly cakes and breads. But there are many "fat-free" or low-fat ingredients which can be used instead:

● Dried fruit purées can replace fat in some cake recipes, as well as contributing valuable nutrients.
● Fruit juice concentrates can be used as a glaze for cakes, sweet breads, cupcakes, and muffins which may look a little dry without any fat.
● Marinating foods in wine, soy sauce, or fruit juice instead of oil will help tenderize and moisten them, as well as improve their appearance and flavor.

TECHNIQUES FOR FAT-FREE COOKING

If you find you need to use a little fat, use oil from a spray, or combine oil with water, fruit juice, or broth and spray it from a plastic spray can or atomizer.

"FRYING"

● To wet-fry, bring a small amount of fat-free liquid (water, broth, wine, cooking liquid from steamed vegetables, meat, or fish) to the boil in a nonstick pan. Reduce the heat to medium-low, then add chopped vegetables, poultry, or meat. Cook, stirring, for 2-15 minutes depending on the ingredients, their size, and the degree of doneness required. Add a little more liquid if necessary.
● Meat containing "hidden" fats, and watery vegetables such as onions, celery, and mushrooms, can be dry-fried without fat in a nonstick skillet over low heat, until tender and even slightly browned.

STEAMING

● Steam vegetables, poultry, or fish in a steamer basket, set over boiling liquid. The liquid can be flavored with herbs and garlic. Save it to use for simmering and stewing.

BROILING AND BARBECUING

● Guaranteed to bring out the best in good quality meats, poultry, fish, and strong-tasting vegetables such as bell peppers, eggplant, and onions. The direct, dry heat quickly seals in juices beneath a crispy exterior.
● Broiling can be used as a flavorful alternative to stewing and simmering vegetables which need pre-cooking before being cooked in a soup, casserole, or oven-baked dish.
● Marinate the foods in blends of herbs, spices, fruit juices, soy sauce, or yogurt, and use the marinade to baste the food during cooking.

ROASTING

● For maximum flavor and moisture, bake fish, poultry, or corn in foil, parchment paper parcels, or sealed roasting bags with wine, citrus juice, or broth. Add herbs, spices, and slivers of vegetables for extra flavor.

COMBINED TECHNIQUES

● Lightly steam vegetables, fish, or poultry, then cook in a sauce.

NON-STICK COOKWARE

Many of these techniques depend on good-quality nonstick cookware to prevent food from sticking and to encourage it to brown without any oil — that way it looks more appetizing. Nonstick cookware has improved beyond belief in recent years. Generally speaking, the more you pay, the better the quality. Many of the newer ranges are dishwasher safe. Some are so durable that they can be used with metal utensils, but most manufacturers recommend using wooden or plastic tools. Use the virtually fat-free diet as an opportunity for treating yourself to some new equipment.

The following are indispensable items in fat-free cooking:

SKILLET — *6-inch*
SKILLET — *9-inch*
SKILLET WITH LID — *12-inch*
RIDGED BROILER PAN, *to use either under the broiler or on top of the stove if you don't have a griddle*
ROASTING PANS — *small and large*
COOKIE SHEETS

FAT-BUSTING TIPS

● Allow soups and stews to cool, then chill. The fat solidifies on the surface and can easily be removed.
● Choose extra-lean cuts of meat and trim off all visible fat. Remove skin from poultry.
● Limit red meats to 2 ounces per serving. Cut in small dice and bulk out with more vegetables and pulses.
● Drain off any fatty liquid from meat after browning.
● Use phyllo or strudel pastry, lightly sprayed with oil, instead of ordinary pastry.
● Use moist, fat-free fillings in sandwiches, then you won't need to use a spread.
● Use evaporated skimmed milk (4% fat) instead of skim milk in dishes such as creamed potatoes. It adds creaminess.
● Use arrowroot, potato starch, and corn-starch to thicken sauces. Unlike wheat flour, they don't need to be mixed with fat.

VIRTUALLY FAT-FREE SNACKS

Even when you're on a drastically fat-reduced diet, you still need tasty snacks. Here are some suggestions:

SUNFLOWER OR PUMPKIN SEEDS (PEPITAS) A tablespoon makes a tasty snack and contains about 2 grams of fat. Good to sprinkle on leafy salads with a low-fat dressing.
BRAZIL NUTS Two whole kernels contain 3.4 grams fat and plenty of carbohydrates, vitamins, and minerals.
FRESH OR DRIED DATES Sweet, energy-boosting, and virtually fat-free.
FRUITS of any description, fresh or dried, are virtually fat-free.
VEGETABLES Crisp sticks of carrot, celery, bell pepper, radishes, jicama, baby corn, and cherry tomatoes are great on their own or with yogurt.
LOW-FAT YOGURT Deliciously creamy and contains only 5% fat.
LOW-FAT CHEESES Virtually fat-free soft cheeses may contain as little as 0.2% fat. Mix them with puréed fruits or honey for extra richness.
FRUITCAKES OR SWEET BREADS These contain far less fat than ordinary cakes or cookies. A small slice contains 1-3 grams of fat.
OAT OR RICE CAKES These contain about 2 grams of fat per cake. Top with chopped banana and low-fat soft cheese.

HIDDEN FATS

Even if we cut down on the amount of fat used in preparation and cooking, there is still the fat already present in the food to consider. The combination of the two affects the overall fat content of the foods we eat. Here are some foods you may not think of as fatty:

Food	Average serving	Fat/g
lean steak	6 ounces	22
canned tomato soup	bowl	6.0
barbecue sauce	2 tbsp	7.0
whole milk	1¼ cups	11.7
peanut butter	2 tbsp	13.0
chocolate	1 ounce	7.4
popcorn	1 ounce	10.7
potato chips	1 ounce	8.5
sponge cake	small slice	26
ice-cream	2 scoops	9.8
avocado pear	half	22

Sauces, salad dressings, and broths are essential to many dishes. Sauces and dressings help moisten food, while broths provide an underlying depth of flavor. These culinary basics can still be part of a virtually fat-free diet.

LOW-FAT CREAMS

Cream is a natural partner to many sweet and savory foods, and an important ingredient in sauces, but it is undeniably high in fat. Fortunately, there are some delicious alternatives which can be used alone or in combination. You can buy virtually fat-free versions of soft cheeses and yogurt, and also a variety of products that are naturally very low in fat:

● **BUTTERMILK** 0.1 grams fat per tbsp. Buttermilk is made from skim milk thickened and soured with a special culture. It is mildly acidic and a good source of calcium. Use in baking or as a drink. It's delicious combined with fruit purée.

● **SMETANA** 1.5 grams fat per tbsp. Similar to sour cream but with a milder flavor. Made from single cream, skim milk, and a souring culture.

● **VERY LOW-FAT CURD CHEESE** 0-1.8 g fat per tbsp. A light, fresh-tasting soft cheese. It has a texture somewhere between cottage cheese and thick yogurt.

● **RICOTTA** 1.7 g fat per tbsp. A clean-tasting fresh cheese made with whey rather than curds. It has a neutral flavor and can be used in both sweet and savory dishes.

Creamy but light low-fat yogurt replaces egg yolks and cream in this smooth, richly flavored ice dessert (recipe page 76).

A mixture of very low-fat curd cheese, buttermilk, and low-fat soft cheese, flavored with a little sugar and grated orange zest makes a delicious alternative to whipped cream (recipe page 70).

VERY LOW-FAT SALAD DRESSINGS

Forget about heavy oily dressings and bring your salad greens to life with nothing more than a squeeze of lemon or lime, a sprinkling of fresh herbs, coarse sea salt, and freshly ground black pepper — the clean, acidic flavors really wake up the palate. Or try one of these very low-fat dressings.

CITRUS DRESSING

1.5 g fat per tbsp

Makes 5 tbsp

$^1/_2$ tsp Dijon mustard
2 tsp olive oil
3 tbsp fresh orange juice
3 tbsp fresh lime juice
pinch of sugar
salt and pepper to taste

Liquidize all the ingredients in a blender until homogenized.

MUSTARD YOGURT DRESSING

0.1 g fat per tbsp

Makes 1 cup

6 tbsp nonfat yogurt
2 tsp Dijon-style mustard
1 tsp wine vinegar
1 tbsp chopped fresh herbs
finely grated zest of $^1/_2$ lemon
freshly ground black pepper

Combine the yogurt, mustard, and vinegar. Stir in the herbs, grated lemon zest, and pepper.

ORIENTAL DRESSING

1.8 g fat per tbsp

Makes 6 tbsp

$1^1/_4$ cups Fat-Free Chicken Broth
(page 16)
2 tbsp minced red onion
$^1/_2$ tsp minced fresh ginger root
$^1/_2$ tsp minced lemon grass
3 sprigs flat-leafed parsley
1 tbsp lime juice
$^1/_2$ tsp salt
2 tsp sesame seeds, toasted and crushed
$^1/_2$ tsp sugar
1 tsp tamari (Japanese soy sauce)
1 tsp dark sesame oil

1 Place the broth, onion, ginger, lemon grass, parsley, lime juice, and salt in a small saucepan. Bring to the boil. Cover and simmer for 5 minutes until reduced, then strain.

2 Place 6 tbsp of the liquid in a blender with the sesame seeds, sugar, tamari, and sesame oil. Liquidize until well homogenized.

15

FAT-FREE BROTHS

Broths are vital to fat-free cooking as they replace the flavor and moisture normally provided by fat. Broths will keep for 4-5 days in the refrigerator, but it's well worth making extra to freeze for later use.

Vegetable broths are not simmered for as long as meat broths because the flavor of some vegetables becomes unpleasant if overcooked. The vegetables should therefore be diced quite finely (about ³/₄ inch square) as this increases the surface area and encourages them to release their nourishing juices more quickly.

LIGHT VEGETABLE BROTH

1.8 g fat per cup
Makes about 3 quarts

This is a good base for light summer soups, stewed vegetables, or poached fish. Use it instead of chicken broth in vegetarian dishes.

1 onion, chopped
10 sprigs parsley, including stalks
2 bay leaves
6 large fresh basil leaves
3-4 fresh thyme sprigs
2 celery stalks, chopped
2 carrots, chopped
2 zucchini, chopped
¹/₂ cup chopped green beans
1 cup chopped large mushrooms
4 tomatoes, quartered
2 strips lemon zest
1 tsp salt
¹/₂ tsp freshly ground black pepper

1 Place the onion and herbs in a large saucepan with about ²/₃ cup water. Cook over a medium-high heat for 4-5 minutes, stirring, until the onion is soft.

2 Add the remaining ingredients, then cover and cook for 10 minutes, stirring occasionally. Pour in enough water to cover by about 2 inches. Bring to the boil, then simmer for 45 minutes.

3 Strain the broth through a fine-meshed sieve, pressing to extract all the liquid. Simmer for a little longer if you want a stronger flavor.

STRONG VEGETABLE BROTH

0.4 g fat per cup
Makes about 3 quarts

This makes a full-bodied broth which is good for hearty soups and casseroles. You can use it wherever you would normally use meat broth.

1 onion, chopped
10 sprigs parsley, including stalks
2 bay leaves
6 sprigs fresh thyme
4 celery stalks with leaves, chopped
3 carrots, chopped
3 tomatoes, quartered
2 leeks, green parts included, quartered lengthwise and chopped
³/₄ cup chopped mushrooms
1 tbsp dried wild mushrooms, soaked in boiling water for 15 minutes
1 eggplant, chopped
1 potato, diced
2 tbsp tamari or shoyu
1 tsp salt
¹/₂ tsp freshly ground black pepper

1 Place the onion and herbs in a large saucepan with about ²/₃ cup water. Cook, stirring, over medium-high heat for 4-5 minutes, until the onion is soft.

2 Add the remaining ingredients. Cover and cook for 10 minutes, stirring occasionally. Pour in enough water to cover by about 2 inches. Bring to the boil, then simmer for 45 minutes.

3 Strain the broth through a fine-meshed sieve or cheesecloth, pressing to extract all the liquid.

FAT-FREE CHICKEN BROTH

0.4 g fat per cup
Makes about 2 ¹/₂ quarts

1 x 5-pound chicken, cut in pieces
1 head of garlic, outer skin removed, clove tips sliced off
3 onions, quartered
2 leeks, split lengthwise
4 carrots, halved
4 celery stalks, halved
10 sprigs parsley
2 bay leaves
2 tsp salt
¹/₂ tsp freshly ground black pepper

1 Place all the ingredients in a large pot with enough water to cover by about 2 inches. Slowly bring to the boil, removing any scum. Simmer over very low heat for 3 hours.

2 Strain through a fine-meshed sieve or cheesecloth into a large bowl, then filter through paper towels. Leave to cool, then place in the refrigerator. When chilled, remove the solid layer of fat.

FAT-FREE MEAT BROTH

0.2 g fat per cup
Makes about 2 ¹/₂ quarts

3 pounds beef or veal bones, cut into large pieces
2 onions, quartered
3 pounds lean shin of beef
1 pound stewing veal
1 pound chicken wings
2 carrots, halved
2 celery stalks with leaves
1 potato
2 tomatoes
10 sprigs parsley
2 tsp salt
¹/₂ tsp freshly ground black pepper

1 Arrange the bones and onions in a nonstick roasting pan. Roast in a preheated oven at 450° for 30 minutes, basting occasionally. Drain off the fat and transfer the bones and onions to a large pot or Dutch oven.

2 Trim any visible fat from the beef and veal, and cut the meat into large chunks. Add to the pot with the remaining ingredients. Pour in enough water to cover by 2 inches. Bring to the boil, half covered, over medium heat. Reduce the heat and simmer very gently for 3 hours, skimming the surface, at intervals, of any impurities.

3 Strain through a fine-meshed sieve or cheesecloth, then filter through paper towels to remove any sediment and fat. Pour into a bowl and leave to cool, then refrigerate. When thoroughly chilled, remove the solid layer of fat from the surface. Store the meat broth in 1-cup containers for later use.

NUTRITIONAL ANALYSES

Nutritional information for each recipe in the book is provided in easy-reference panels. The nutritional figures are per serving of the recipe in each case, and do not include any serving suggestions that may be included in the introduction or at the end of a recipe, unless specifically stated otherwise in the nutritional panel. These analyses have been compiled as accurately as possible, but the nutritional content of foods will vary depending on their source.

As well as specifying the number of calories per serving, the nutritional analysis also gives the overall fat content, which is then broken down into the three main types of fat: saturates, monounsaturates, and polyunsaturates. Your intake of saturated fats should be kept low for good health.

The analysis also gives the percentage of total calories from fat, which should be no more than 30-35% for good health, as well as the percentage of calories from saturated fats. In a healthy diet, this should not exceed 10%.

The recommended daily intake of dietary fiber is between 12 and 18 g, so the figure given in the nutritional analyses indicates how much fiber each recipe can contribute to your daily total.

Figures for the sodium content of each recipe are also included. This figure does not include any salt or other seasoning that may be added to the recipe during preparation and cooking, other than where specified amounts are stated.

Where a nutritional analysis states that a recipe is a good source of a particular vitamin, mineral, or other nutrient, this indicates that a serving of the recipe will make a significant contribution to the recommended daily allowance (RDA) of the nutrients.

A GUIDE TO THE RECIPES

● All spoon measurements refer to American Standard measuring spoons, and all measurements given are for level spoons unless otherwise stated.

● The cooking times for all the recipes in this book are based on the oven or broiler being preheated.

● All eggs used in the recipes are medium (weighing 21 ounces per dozen) eggs.

KEY TO SYMBOLS

 Suitable for freezing.

 Suitable for cooking in a microwave oven.

 Suitable for vegetarians.

Please note that the term vegetarian applies to lacto-ovo vegetarians, i.e. people who eat eggs and dairy products but not meat, fish, and poultry, nor any products derived from these foods.

CHAPTER ONE

VEGETABLES

Containing the merest trace of fat, vegetables take on a justifiably high profile in a virtually fat-free diet. They are a vital source of fiber, vitamins, and minerals. Yellow and orange varieties, such as carrots, sweet potatoes, and butternut squash, are bursting with beta-carotene, a powerful antioxidant known to help prevent cancer. Dark green leafy vegetables also contain beta-carotene, as well as calcium, iron, and vitamin C. Vegetables offer an infinite variety of tastes, textures, and flavors. Depending on type, the buds, leaves, stems, flowers, and roots of vegetables are all at our disposal to be turned into delicious and satisfying main meals, appetizers, and snacks.

CARROT, TOMATO, &
PEPPER SOUP

Two colorful purées are swirled together to make a robustly flavored and filling soup. Serve with warm crusty bread.

Preparation time: 20 minutes

Cooking time: 30 minutes

Serves 4

2 large red bell peppers
2 large tomatoes
1 garlic clove, unpeeled
¹/₂-inch piece fresh ginger root, minced
2-3 fresh thyme sprigs
1 onion, chopped
1 small leek, split lengthwise and chopped
1 cup (8 ounces) thinly sliced carrots
¹/₄ cup (2 ounces) diced potato
3³/₄ cups Fat-Free Chicken Broth (page 16)
or Strong Vegetable Broth (page 16)
salt and freshly ground black pepper
squeeze of lemon juice
toasted sesame seeds, to garnish

1 Preheat the oven to 425°. Place the bell peppers, tomatoes, and garlic in a roasting pan. Roast the garlic for about 10 minutes, until soft. Roast the bell peppers and tomatoes for a further 10 minutes, until the skins are blackened and blistered.

2 Meanwhile, place the ginger, thyme, and half the onion in a saucepan with the leek, carrots, potato, and ²/₃ cup of the broth. Wet-fry over medium heat until the onion is soft. Add a further 2 cups of broth and seasoning. Cover and simmer over low heat until the carrots are tender.

3 Remove the skin, core, and seeds from the bell peppers, then roughly chop the flesh. Peel the tomatoes and garlic, reserving any juice. Transfer to a blender or food processor with the remaining onion and broth, and season with salt and pepper. Purée until smooth, then transfer to a small saucepan. Add a squeeze of lemon juice, then simmer over low heat for a few minutes.

4 Purée the carrot mixture, return to the pan, and check the seasoning. Reheat gently.

5 Pour the carrot soup into warm bowls. Swirl the tomato and pepper soup into the center. Garnish with sesame seeds.

NUTRITIONAL ANALYSIS

(figures are per serving)

Calories = 74
Fat = 0.8g
of which saturates = 0.2g
     monounsaturates = 0.1g
     polyunsaturates = 0.5g
Protein = 2.3g
Carbohydrate = 15.4g
Dietary fiber = 4.5g
Sodium = 0.02g

Percentage of total calories from fat = 10%
of which saturates = 2%
Good source of vitamins A & C

MINTED ZUCCHINI & PEA
SOUP

A refreshing soup, ideal for a summer lunch.

Preparation time: 25 minutes
Cooking time: 30 minutes
Serves 6

2 shallots, chopped
1 garlic clove, minced
2 tbsp minced fresh mint
3³/₄ cups Fat-Free Chicken Broth (page 16)
1¹/₂ cups (9 ounces) mixed green and yellow
zucchini, finely diced
¹/₂ cup shelled peas (about 9 ounces unshelled)
¹/₂ cup corn kernels (from 1 large cob)
1 small potato, diced
squeeze of lemon juice
salt and freshly ground black pepper
small sprigs of mint, to garnish

1 Place the shallots, garlic, and mint in a nonstick saucepan with a ladleful of broth. Wet-fry over medium heat for 4-5 minutes, or until the shallots are softened.

2 Add the zucchini, the shelled peas, corn, potato, and another ladleful of broth to moisten. Cover and cook over medium heat for 10 minutes, until the vegetables are beginning to soften slightly.

3 Add the remaining broth and bring to the boil. Season to taste, then simmer for about 10 minutes, until the vegetables are just tender.

4 Leave about one-third of the mixture in the pan, then purée the rest until smooth. (If you prefer a completely smooth soup, purée all of it.)

5 Return the mixture to the pan and reheat gently. Add a squeeze of lemon juice to sharpen the flavor, and check the seasoning.

6 Pour into warm bowls. Garnish each serving with a sprig of mint. Serve with warm crusty bread or crackers.

VARIATIONS
● Use chopped asparagus in place of the zucchini.
● Use fresh coriander (cilantro) or flat-leafed parsley in place of the mint.

COOK'S TIP
● If you are short of time, use frozen corn and peas.

NUTRITIONAL ANALYSIS

(figures are per serving)

Calories = 60	Protein = 3.4g
Fat = 0.9g	Carbohydrate = 10.1g
of which saturates = 0.1g	Dietary fiber = 2.0g
monounsaturates = 0.1g	Sodium = 3 mg
polyunsaturates = 0.4g	

Percentage of total calories from fat = 14% , of which saturates = 2%
Good source of vitamin C

GREEN PEPPER &
AVOCADO DIP

*Serve this colorful dip as an appetizer or snack,
or spooned over broiled fish or chicken.*

Preparation time: 20 minutes

Cooking time: 10 minutes

Serves 6

2 green bell peppers, halved, cored, and seeded
$^1/_2$ small fresh green chili, finely chopped
$^1/_2$ small avocado
2 garlic cloves, crushed
3 green onions (scallions), green parts
included, chopped
finely grated rind and juice of 1 lime
4 tbsp chopped fresh coriander (cilantro)
salt and freshly ground black pepper
4 small wheat tortillas, to serve
lime wedge and a sprig of fresh
coriander (cilantro), to garnish

1 Place the bell peppers cut side downward in a broiler pan. Broil under very high heat for 10 minutes, until blackened. Peel off the skin and roughly chop the flesh.

2 Place the bell peppers and the remaining ingredients in a food processor or blender. Purée until smooth. Check the seasoning and add more lime juice if necessary.

3 Spoon into a serving bowl, then cover and chill. Garnish with lime and coriander (cilantro) just before serving. Serve with the wheat tortillas and chunks of crisp, raw vegetables.

NUTRITIONAL ANALYSIS

(figures are per serving)

Calories = 104
Fat = 2.2g
of which saturates = 0.5g
    monounsaturates = 1.04g
    polyunsaturates = 0.4g
Protein = 3.6g
Carbohydrate = 18.8g
Dietary fiber = 2.1g
Sodium = 0.16g

Percentage of total calories from fat = 19%
of which saturates = 4%
Good source of vitamin C

EGGPLANT & TOMATO
CROSTINI

Preparation time: 30 minutes
Cooking time: 2 hours 55 minutes

Serves 4

3 plum tomatoes, halved crosswise
pinch of dark brown sugar
pinch of fennel seeds (optional)
freshly ground black pepper
1 large eggplant
2 garlic cloves, unpeeled
1 small fresh red chili
¼ cup minced red onion
2 tsp sun-dried tomato paste or tomato paste
1 tsp tamari (Japanese soy sauce)
1 tsp finely-grated lemon rind
½ tsp coriander (cilantro) seeds,
toasted and crushed
½-inch piece fresh ginger root, minced
salt
1 small French stick, thickly sliced
chopped fresh flat-leafed parsley, to garnish

1 Pack the tomatoes, cut side upward, in a single layer in a shallow ovenproof dish into which they fit snugly. Sprinkle with the sugar, fennel seeds (if using), and pepper. Roast in a preheated oven at 275° for 1½-2 hours, until beginning to shrivel. Remove from the dish with a slotted spoon, cut in half, and set aside.

2 Raise the oven temperature to 425°. Prick the eggplant in several places. Place in a roasting pan with the garlic and chilies. Roast until soft. The garlic and chilies will need 10-15 minutes, the eggplant 40-45 minutes.

3 Remove the skin and seeds from the chili, and the skin from the garlic. Peel the eggplant. Place in a food processor or blender with the onion,

tomato paste, tamari, lemon rind, coriander seeds, ginger, and salt and pepper. Process to a chunky purée.

4 Reduce the oven temperature to 300°. Spread the bread in a single layer on a cookie sheet and toast for 10 minutes until slightly crisp.

5 To serve, spread the toast with the eggplant purée, top with pieces of tomato, and sprinkle with parsley.

VARIATION
● Use slivers of raw tomato or red bell pepper instead of oven-dried tomatoes.

COOK'S TIP
● Serve at room temperature to allow the flavors to come through.

NUTRITIONAL ANALYSIS

(figures are per serving)

Calories = 146
Fat = 1.8g
of which saturates = 0.4g
    monounsaturates = 0.4g
    polyunsaturates = 0.6g
Protein = 5.7g
Carbohydrate = 29.4g
Dietary fiber = 4.6g
Sodium = 0.32g

Percentage of total calories from fat = 11%
of which saturates = 3%
Good source of vitamin C

GREEN BEAN &
KOHLRABI SALAD

ORIENTAL SALAD

A crisp and colorful salad of crunchy vegetables with a lemony yogurt dressing. Serve with rye bread as an appetizer or light entrée.

Preparation time: 30 minutes
Cooking time: 3 minutes
Serves 4

Serve as an appetizer or as an accompaniment to broiled or stir-fried fish, seafood, or poultry.

Preparation time: 15 minutes
Serves 4

*6 ounces fine green beans, trimmed and cut into
1 1/2-inch pieces
3 small kohlrabi, weighing about 4 ounces each
2 small carrots, thinly sliced
1/2 yellow bell pepper, seeded and finely diced
3 green onions (scallions),
green parts included, sliced
coarse sea salt and freshly ground black pepper
1 tbsp pumpkin seeds (pepitas)
1 tbsp chopped fresh dill
6 tbsp Mustard Yogurt Dressing (page 15)*

1 Place the beans in a steamer over boiling water and steam for 2-3 minutes until just tender but still crunchy. Alternatively, cook them in a microwave oven. Allow to cool.

2 Peel and thinly slice the kohlrabi. Stack a few slices at a time and cut into matchstick strips.

3 Combine the beans, kohlrabi, carrots, bell pepper, and green onions (scallions) in a large bowl and season.

4 Divide the mixture between four serving plates. Sprinkle with pumpkin seeds (pepitas). Stir the dill into the dressing and spoon a little over each plate.

COOK'S TIPS
● Kohlrabi is a neglected vegetable which deserves to be used more often. It has a unique, slightly peppery flavor and the crunch and juiciness of an apple.
● Be sure to use small kohlrabi since the larger specimens tend to be tough and woody.

*10 ounces mixed young oriental greens such as
mustard greens, bok choy, tatsoi, and mizuna
1/3 Chinese (Napa) cabbage, cut lengthwise
1/2 cup snow-peas, trimmed and thinly sliced
diagonally
1/3 cup brown mushrooms, very thinly sliced
2 green onions (scallions), cut crosswise into
1-inch strips
1/2 cup cold boiled rice
6 tbsp Oriental Dressing (page 15)
1 tsp toasted sesame seeds*

1 Tear the greens and bok choy stalks into bite-sized pieces. Slice the Chinese cabbage crosswise.

2 Arrange all the greens and vegetables attractively on individual serving plates with a small mound of rice in the center.

3 Spoon the dressing over the top and sprinkle with the sesame seeds.

NUTRITIONAL ANALYSIS
(figures are per serving)

Calories = 78	Protein = 4.5g
Fat = 1.9g	Carbohydrate = 11.1g
of which saturates = 0.3g	Dietary fiber = 3.0g
monounsaturates = 0.4g	Sodium = 0.05g
polyunsaturates = 0.8g	

Percentage of total calories from fat = 22%
of which saturates = 3%
Good source of vitamin A & folic acid

NUTRITIONAL ANALYSIS
(figures are per serving)

Calories = 96	Protein = 4.6g
Kilojoules = 401	Carbohydrate = 12.8g
	Dietary fiber = 5.7g
Fat = 3.2g	Sodium = 0.09g
of which saturates = 0.5g	
monounsaturates = 0.9g	
polyunsaturates = 1.5g	

Percentage of total calories from fat = 30%
of which saturates = 4%
Good source of vitamins A & C, folic acid, & iron

PAPAYA & BEAN SPROUT
SALAD

Full of contrasting flavors and textures, this salad makes a delicious appetizer or low-calorie lunch.

Preparation time: 15 minutes

Serves 2

*1 large, ripe papaya
squeeze of lime juice
7 ounces (about 4 handfuls) green and red salad
leaves such as frisée, romaine, lamb's lettuce, and
oakleaf lettuce, torn into bite-sized pieces
^{1}/$_2$ ounce (small handful) arugula
^{1}/$_2$ small cucumber, very thinly sliced
^{1}/$_2$ cup bean sprouts
1^1/$_2$ tbsp Citrus Dressing (page 15)*

1 Halve the papaya lengthwise and scoop out the seeds, reserving a few for garnish. Using a small sharp knife, carefully remove the skin. Slice the flesh lengthwise into thin segments. Place in a shallow dish, and sprinkle with a squeeze of lime juice.

2 Arrange the leaves on individual plates. Scatter the cucumber, bean sprouts, and papaya over the top, and sprinkle with the reserved papaya seeds.

3 Spoon the dressing over the salad and serve at once with crackers or crusty bread.

VARIATIONS
● Add a tablespoon of cottage cheese for extra protein.
● Use muskmelon or mango instead of papaya.
● Replace the cucumber with thinly sliced mushrooms.

NUTRITIONAL ANALYSIS
(figures are per serving)

Calories = 109
Fat = 2.2g
of which saturates = 0.3g
monounsaturates = 0.9g
polyunsaturates = 0.6g
Protein = 3.2g
Carbohydrate = 20.4g
Dietary fiber = 6.4g
Sodium = 0.02g

Percentage of total calories from fat = 18%
of which saturates = 3%
Good source of beta-carotene, folic acid, vitamin C, & iron

STEAMED BROCCOLI
WITH LEMON & PARMESAN

The minutest amount of Parmesan cheese and fresh-tasting lemon rind make this a flavorful side dish. Try it when you are tired of plainly cooked green vegetables.

Preparation time: 15 minutes

Cooking time: 5 minutes

Serves 4

1¹/₂ cups (12 ounces) broccoli
¹/₂ tsp olive oil
1 garlic clove, thinly sliced
coarsely grated rind of ¹/₂ lemon
sea salt and freshly ground black pepper
2 tbsp chopped flat-leafed parsley
1 ounce Parmesan cheese,
shaved into wafer-thin curls

1 Divide the broccoli into even-sized flowerets. Trim the woody end off the central stalk and cut the stalk into thin diagonal slices.

2 Transfer the flowerets and sliced stalk to a steamer basket. Steam over boiling water for 1 minute, until just tender.

3 Heat the oil in a nonstick skillet. Add the garlic and gently fry over medium-low heat for 30 seconds until just colored — do not allow it to burn. Add the broccoli, lemon rind, salt, pepper, and parsley. Toss for a few seconds, then add the Parmesan cheese. Toss again, then transfer to a heated dish, and serve immediately.

4 Serve the broccoli with baked potatoes to accompany fish, meat, or chicken.

VARIATIONS
● Use a mixture of broccoli and cauliflower flowerets.
    ● For a spicier flavor, sprinkle with dried red pepper flakes and omit the lemon rind.

ROASTED PAPRIKA
POTATOES

Serve these crispy cubes of oven-roasted potato as a side dish with red meats, chicken, fish, or with a vegetarian entrée.

Preparation time: 25 minutes

Cooking time: 45 minutes

Serves 4

1³/₄ pounds potatoes
1 tbsp chopped fresh rosemary
1 tbsp olive oil
1 tsp paprika
salt and freshly ground black pepper

1 Peel the potatoes and slightly trim the ends and sides to straighten. Cut into ³/₄-inch cubes.

2 Bring a saucepan of salted water to the boil. Boil the potatoes for 5 minutes, until just tender. Alternatively, cook them in a microwave oven. Tip into a colander and drain, shaking the colander to roughen the edges of the cubes, so that they become crisp when roasted.

3 Combine the rosemary, oil, paprika, and salt and pepper. Add to the potatoes and toss carefully to coat.

4 Arrange the potatoes in a single layer in a nonstick roasting pan. Roast in a preheated oven at 400°, tossing occasionally, for 35 minutes, until golden brown.

NUTRITIONAL ANALYSIS
(figures are per serving)

Calories = 178
Fat = 3.3 g
of which saturates = 0.4g
    monounsaturates = 2.0g
    polyunsaturates = 0.5g
Protein = 4.3g
Carbohydrate = 34.9g
Dietary fiber = 3.2g
Sodium = 0.01g

Percentage of total calories from fat = 16%
of which saturates = 2%
Good source of vitamin C

COOK'S TIP
● Make sure the roasting pan is large enough. If the potato cubes are crowded, they will steam in their own moisture rather than roast.

MIXED ROOT
VEGETABLES

Serve this as a side dish with broiled meats or chicken.

Preparation time: 35 minutes

Cooking time: 1¹/₂ hours

Serves 8

2 onions, thickly sliced
vegetable oil spray
14 ounces potatoes
1 pound 10 ounces mixed root vegetables such as
turnip, parsnip, celery root (celeriac), carrot,
jicama, yucca, and rutabaga
2 tbsp chopped fresh rosemary
1 tbsp chopped fresh thyme
salt and freshly ground black pepper
1¹/₂ cups Fat-Free Chicken Broth (page 16) or
Strong Vegetable Broth (page 16)
2 tsp butter
chopped fresh parsley

1 Arrange the sliced onions in a single layer in the bottom of a nonstick roasting pan. Lightly spray with oil. Roast in a preheated oven at 475° for 10-12 minutes. Remove the pan from the oven and reduce the temperature to 375°.

2 Peel and thinly slice the potatoes and the other root vegetables. Lightly spray a 2-quart ovenproof dish with oil. Layer the onions and other vegetables in the dish, sprinkling each layer with the fresh herbs, salt, and pepper.

NUTRITIONAL ANALYSIS
(figures are per serving)

Calories = 90
Fat = 1.8g
of which saturates = 0.8g
    monounsaturates = 0.4g
    polyunsaturates = 0.3g
Protein = 2.4g
Carbohydrate = 16.9g
Dietary fiber = 4.4g
Sodium = 0.04g

Percentage of total calories from fat = 18%
of which saturates = 8%
Good source of vitamins A & C, & folic acid

3 Pour in the broth. Cover tightly with foil and bake for 1 hour, or until tender. Remove the foil, dot the vegetables with the butter, and bake for another 20 minutes to brown the top.

BROILING VEGETABLES

If you are following a virtually fat-free diet, broiling or oven-roasting vegetables is a wonderful way of preparing them. The best candidates for broiling are bell peppers, red onions, zucchini, eggplant, and tomatoes. If you use a nonstick roasting pan, you will not normally need to add any oil, but if the vegetables start to look dry, you may need to moisten them lightly with oil from a spray. To create that mouthwatering, charbroiled look, vegetables need to be subjected to intense heat. You can do this in a very hot oven or covered barbecue, or alternatively under a hot broiler or over hot coals.

Eaten hot, cold, or at room temperature, broiled vegetables make a delicious side dish, vegetarian main meal, or salad. They do not require any oily dressing since they produce their own juices, although a sprinkling of good quality vinegar or lemon juice adds a pleasantly sharp note. Pungent herbs such as rosemary, basil, and thyme are also good to use.

Broiling or oven-roasting are particularly useful techniques for vegetables that need softening before being added to a stew or soup. Wet-frying produces satisfactory results, but broiling provides the finished dish with the rich, mellow flavor usually supplied by fat.

RATATOUILLE

Preparation time: 20 minutes
Cooking time: 40 minutes
Serves 6

olive oil spray
1 large eggplant, cut crosswise into 1 inch thick slices
2 cups large, flat-cap mushrooms, quartered
2 zucchini, halved lengthwise
2 large red bell peppers, halved, cored, and seeded
2-2$^{1}/_{2}$ cups Fat-Free Vegetable Broth (page 16)
2-3 sprigs of fresh thyme
1 tbsp chopped fresh rosemary
1 onion, minced
2 garlic cloves, minced
1 pound plum tomatoes, peeled and chopped
2 tbsp tamari (Japanese soy sauce)
2 slivers of lemon rind
$^{1}/_{2}$ tsp sugar
salt and freshly ground black pepper
pinch of dried red pepper flakes
2 tbsp flat-leafed parsley, trimmed and chopped

1 Lightly spray the eggplant, mushrooms, and zucchini all over with cooking oil from a spray can. Arrange in a nonstick broiler pan with the bell peppers, cut-side downward. Broil for 10-12 minutes, turning halfway through the cooking time, until they are beginning to blacken. Cut all the vegetables into even-sized chunks and set aside.

NUTRITIONAL ANALYSIS
(figures are per serving)

Calories = 110	Protein = 5.1g
Fat = 1.7g	Carbohydrate = 20.0g
of which saturates = 0.3g	Dietary fiber = 6.3g
monounsaturates = 04g	Sodium = 0.33g
polyunsaturates = 0.7g	

Percentage of total calories from fat = 14%, of which saturates = 3%
Good source of vitamins A, C, E, & B vitamins

2 Pour ²⁄₃ cup of the broth into a heavy-based casserole or pan over medium heat. Add the thyme, rosemary, onion, and garlic. Wet-fry for 5 minutes, until the onion is soft.

3 Add the tomatoes and their juice, tamari, lemon rind, sugar, salt and pepper, and 1¼ cups of the broth. Bring to the boil, then simmer over low heat for 10 minutes, stirring occasionally, until slightly thickened.

4 Add the broiled vegetables, red pepper flakes, and all but 1 tbsp of the parsley. Bring to the boil, then cover and simmer for 10 minutes, adding a little more broth if necessary. Check the seasoning, and garnish with the remaining parsley before serving.

5 Serve at room temperature with some crusty bread, or hot with rice or cracked wheat as a light meal.

VARIATION
● Replace the eggplant or mushrooms with extra zucchini or peppers.

SPINACH & BELL PEPPER
FRITTATA

Preparation time: 20 minutes
Cooking time: 15 minutes

Serves 6

6 ounces (about 4 cups uncooked)
young spinach leaves
2 large eggs
4 egg whites (from large eggs)
³⁄₄ tsp ground turmeric
4 tbsp Fat-Free Chicken Broth (page 16) or
Strong Vegetable Broth (page 16)
3 green onions (scallions),
green parts included, minced
3 tbsp finely diced red bell pepper
2 cups cooked new potatoes, cut into small chunks
½-inch piece fresh ginger root, finely chopped
pinch of red pepper flakes
¼ tsp olive oil
¼ tsp salt
freshly ground black pepper

1 Wash the spinach thoroughly, remove any coarse stems, and roughly chop the leaves. Place in a saucepan without any extra water. Cook over medium heat for 2-3 minutes, or until just tender. Drain, squeeze dry, and place in a small bowl.

2 In a large bowl, lightly beat the whole eggs with the whites and ¼ tsp of the turmeric.

3 Pour the broth into a nonstick 9½-10-inch skillet with the green onions (scallions), bell pepper, potatoes, ginger, red pepper flakes, and remaining turmeric. Wet-fry over medium heat for a minute or two, then mix with the spinach in the bowl.

4 Heat the oil in the pan, then pour in a thin layer of the egg mixture, and allow to set. Add the spinach mixture and remaining egg, stirring to distribute the spinach evenly. Cook over medium heat for about 5 minutes, until almost set.

5 Place under a preheated medium-hot broiler for a few minutes to brown the top.

6 Cut the frittata into wedges and serve warm with crusty bread, shredded lettuce, and sliced cherry tomatoes.

COOK'S TIP
● Normally made with whole eggs, the fat content of this frittata is reduced to a minimum by using a third of the usual amount of egg yolks.

NUTRITIONAL ANALYSIS
(figures are per serving)

Calories = 101
Fat = 4.0g
of which saturates = 1.1g
    monounsaturates = 1.6g
    polyunsaturates = 0.7g

Protein = 8.7g
Carbohydrate = 8.2g
Dietary fiber = 2.1g
Sodium = 0.17g

Percentage of total calories from fat = 35% , of which saturates = 10%
Good source of vitamin A

BRAISED
SPRING VEGETABLES

*Serve these crunchy, tender young vegetables with
pasta as a vegetarian entrée.*

Preparation time: 40 minutes

Cooking time: 10 minutes

Serves 6

2 tbsp sunflower margarine
6 large green onions (scallions), trimmed and
halved lengthwise
2-3 sprigs of thyme
sea salt
4 ounces ($^3/_4$ cup) baby carrots
$^2/_3$ cup baby corn cobs
$^3/_4$ cup fine green beans, trimmed
1 cup baby asparagus tips
$^3/_4$ cup broccoli flowerets, cut into small pieces
about $1^1/_2$ inches across
$^1/_2$ cup sugar snap peas
$^1/_2$ cup shelled young fava beans,
outer skins removed
3 tbsp chopped fresh mixed herbs such as
flat-leafed parsley, chives, and basil
1 tbsp lemon juice
freshly ground black pepper
1 pound 2 ounces (4 cups) pasta shapes, to serve

1 Have ready a large pan of boiling salted water over which you have fitted a steamer basket with a lid.

2 Melt half the margarine in a large nonstick skillet. Add the onions, thyme, sea salt, and $^3/_4$ cup water. Bring to the boil, cover, and simmer for 5 minutes.

3 Meanwhile, steam the carrots, corn, and beans together for 2 minutes. Add them to the onions in the pan and leave to simmer. Next, steam the asparagus and broccoli together for 1 minute, then add these to the pan containing the other vegetables, and continue to simmer. Finally, steam the sugar snap peas and shelled fava beans together for 1 minute, then add these to the pan as well.

4 When all the vegetables are in the pan, stir in the remaining margarine, the herbs, and lemon juice. Season with pepper and a little more salt if necessary. Cover and cook for a further minute.

5 Cook the pasta according to the instructions on the package and serve with the vegetables.

COOK'S TIP
● Make sure the pasta is ready to be served by the time you have finished cooking the vegetables.

NUTRITIONAL ANALYSIS

(figures are per serving including pasta)

Calories = 150
Fat = 4.5g
of which saturates = 0.9g
     monounsaturates = 0.9g
     polyunsaturates = 2.2g
Protein = 7.4g
Carbohydrate = 21.5g
Dietary fiber = 3.7g
Sodium = 0.06g

Percentage of total calories from fat = 27%
of which saturates = 6%
Good source of vitamins A & C, & folic acid

≋ BEETS & GREENS
WITH CORIANDER SAUCE

This makes a colorful and substantial vegetarian entrée served with cooked soft grains such as cracked wheat or buckwheat.

Preparation time: 30 minutes

Cooking time: 1 hour 35 minutes

Serves 2-3

3 (about 9 ounces) uncooked small red beets
1/2 cup nonfat plain yogurt
2 tbsp chopped fresh coriander (cilantro)
1 garlic clove, crushed
salt and freshly ground black pepper
6 ounces (about 3 cups) trimmed greens such as collard greens, beet greens, turnip greens, or cabbage, cut into ribbons
1 tsp sunflower oil
4 tbsp Strong Vegetable Broth (page 16)
finely grated rind of 1/2 lemon

1 Wash the beets, taking care not to tear the skins. Dry thoroughly and wrap loosely in heavy-duty aluminum foil. Roast in a preheated oven at 400° for 1-1 1/2 hours, until tender. Alternatively, they can be cooked in a covered container in a microwave oven.

2 Meanwhile, place the yogurt in a small bowl and mix with the coriander (cilantro), garlic, and salt and pepper to taste.

3 Carefully peel the beets and cut into quarters lengthwise. Keep them warm while you cook the greens.

4 Heat a nonstick wok or skillet over medium-high heat. Add the greens, sunflower oil, broth, and lemon rind, and wet-fry for 3-4 minutes, until just tender and still bright green.

5 Arrange the greens and beets on warmed serving plates. Top with a spoonful of the coriander sauce.

VARIATION

● Replace some or all of the greens with stir-fried leeks or steamed green beans.

NUTRITIONAL ANALYSIS

(figures are per serving)

Calories = 111
Fat = 2.7 g
of which saturates = 0.3g
   monounsaturates = 0.4g
   polyunsaturates = 1.6g

Protein = 7.2g
Carbohydrate = 15.5g
Dietary fiber = 8.8 g
Sodium = 0.1g

Percentage of total calories from fat = 22%, of which saturates = 2%
Good source of vitamins A & C, folic acid, & iron

STUFFED BELL
PEPPERS

With a vibrantly flavored stuffing of rice, lemon, and diced zucchini, these colorful peppers make a satisfying vegetarian entrée.

Preparation time: 50 minutes

Cooking time: 1 hour 15 minutes

Serves 4 (makes 4 peppers)

FOR THE STUFFING
2 tsp olive oil
2 tbsp Strong Vegetable Broth (page 16)
1 onion, minced
²/₃ cup long-grain rice
2 tbsp lemon juice
¹/₂ cup water
1 zucchini, very finely diced
3 tbsp chopped flat-leafed parsley
1 tbsp chopped fresh mint
¹/₄ tsp ground cinnamon
¹/₄ tsp ground allspice
salt and freshly ground black pepper

4 small red or yellow bell peppers
³/₄ cup tomato juice
salt and freshly ground black pepper
sprigs of flat-leafed parsley, to garnish

1 To make the stuffing, heat the oil and the broth in a small saucepan over medium heat. Add the onion, then cover and wet-fry for 4 minutes until soft.

2 Stir in the rice, lemon juice, and water. Cover and simmer for 10 minutes.

3 Mix the diced zucchini with the rice and cook for a further 2 minutes. Add a little more water or broth if the mixture becomes too dry. Stir in the parsley, mint, cinnamon, allspice, and salt and pepper.

4 With a small pointed knife, cut a circle around the top of the bell peppers, slightly wider than the base of the stem. Remove and discard the stem and core, reserving the tops to be used as "lids." Remove the seeds and ribs.

5 Fill the bell peppers with the rice mixture, leaving a little space for the rice to expand. Cover the tops with the lids.

6 Stand the bell peppers upright in a heavy-based saucepan into which they fit snugly. Add the tomato juice and enough water to come one-third of the way up their sides. Season with salt and pepper. Cover tightly and bring to the boil, then simmer for 30 minutes over very low heat.

7 Transfer the bell peppers to a serving dish and garnish with parsley sprigs. Spoon some of the cooking liquid over the peppers and serve the remainder in a jug. Serve the bell peppers with a bowl of nonfat plain yogurt and hunks of crusty bread for mopping up the juices.

VARIATION
● Use cracked wheat or buckwheat as a stuffing instead of the rice.

NUTRITIONAL ANALYSIS

(figures are per serving)

Calories = 206
Fat = 3.4g
of which saturates = 0.6g
    monounsaturates = 1.4g
    polyunsaturates = 0.9g
Protein = 5.2g
Carbohydrate = 41.4g
Dietary fiber = 4.1g
Sodium = 0.11g

Percentage of total calories from fat = 15%
of which saturates = 3%
Good source of vitamins A, C, E, & B vitamins

EASTERN
MEDITERRANEAN
CASSEROLE

Bursting with color and flavor, this comforting casserole makes an excellent entrée for a fall dinner.

Preparation time: 25 minutes

Cooking time: 45 minutes

Serves 4-6

1 tsp cumin seeds
2 tsp coriander (cilantro) seeds
1 tbsp sesame seeds
2 tsp dried oregano
1 tsp vegetable oil
1 onion, chopped
3 garlic cloves, finely chopped
1 green chili, seeded and chopped
1¹/₂ cups Strong Vegetable Broth (page 16)
1 cup butternut squash or pumpkin flesh, cut into chunks
1 small eggplant, cut into chunks
1 red bell pepper, cut into squares
6 ounces green beans, chopped
6 ounces small new potatoes, unpeeled
14-ounce can peeled, chopped tomatoes
salt and freshly ground black pepper
6 ounces shredded green cabbage

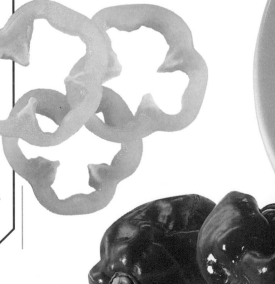

1 Place the seeds in a small heavy-based pan without any oil. Heat until the aroma rises. Add the oregano and dry-fry for a few more seconds. Remove from the heat, crush with a pestle and mortar, and set aside.

2 Heat the oil in a heavy-based nonstick casserole. Gently fry the onion for a few minutes over medium-low heat until translucent. Add the garlic, chili, and 2 tbsp of the stock. Fry for 3 more minutes until soft. Stir in the seed mixture.

3 Add the squash, eggplant, bell pepper, beans, potatoes, and tomatoes. Bring to the boil, then cover and cook over medium-low heat for 10 minutes.

4 Pour in the remaining broth and season with salt and pepper. Bring to the boil then cover and simmer for 20 minutes. Add more broth if the mixture starts to look dry.

5 Stir in the cabbage and cook for 2-3 minutes until just wilted but still bright green. Serve immediately with plainly cooked rice or cracked wheat.

VARIATION
● Use 1 cup (8 ounces) mushrooms in place of the eggplant.

COOK'S TIP
● The toasted crushed seeds act as a thickener and also add a wonderfully earthy flavor to the dish.

NUTRITIONAL ANALYSIS
(figures are per serving)

Calories = 128
Fat = 2.7 g
of which saturates = 0.4g
      monounsaturates = 0.7g
      polyunsaturates = 1.2g
Protein = 5.5g
Carbohydrate = 22.4g
Dietary fiber = 5.8g
Sodium = 0.05g

Percentage of total calories from fat = 19%
of which saturates = 3%
Good source of vitamins A, C, & E,
folic acid & iron

CHAPTER TWO

POULTRY, MEAT, & GAME

*C*hicken, meat, and game contain valuable nutrients and add satisfying flavor to meals.
The drawback is that these foods are a major source of cholesterol and saturated fats —
the substances implicated in heart disease. Chosen with care, however, they can still have a place in a
virtually fat-free diet. Part of the solution is to eat the meat and not the fat. But even if you choose
lean cuts or trim visible fat from standard cuts, there is still the problem of the hidden fat, or marbling,
so you'll need to cut down on serving sizes too. Think of meat as an accompaniment to vegetables,
grains, or pasta, rather than the other way round. Choosing the variety is also important — poultry is
lowest in fat, the white meat containing less fat than the dark meat. Game meats, such as venison,
buffalo, and rabbit, are very lean.

BEEF & MUSHROOM
PHYLLO PARCELS

*These spicy little phyllo parcels are ideal to serve with drinks or as
a snack. Phyllo dough can be found in Greek stores;
strudel dough can be substituted.*

Preparation time: 40 minutes

Cooking time: 30 minutes

Makes 12

4 tbsp Fat-Free Meat Broth (page 17)
¹/₃ cup minced onion
1 garlic clove, finely chopped
¹/₂ tsp ground allspice
¹/₄ tsp ground cinnamon
freshly ground black pepper
²/₃ cup lean ground sirloin steak
1 cup finely chopped mushrooms
finely grated rind of 1 lemon
salt
*4 sheets phyllo or studel dough,
measuring 10 ³/₄ x 10 inches*
olive oil spray

1 Place the broth, onion, garlic, allspice, cinnamon, and pepper in a nonstick skillet. Wet-fry over medium-low heat for 2-3 minutes, until the onion is soft.

2 Add the beef and mushrooms. Raise the heat to medium and cook for a further 5-6 minutes, until the mushrooms are cooked. Stir in the lemon rind and season with salt. Allow to cool.

3 Cut the phyllo dough into 12 long strips measuring 3¹/₂ x 10 inches.

4 Lightly spray one strip with oil. Place about 2 level tablespoons of the filling in the bottom left-hand corner of a strip, and fold over diagonally to form a triangle. Continue to fold until you reach the end of the strip. Repeat with the remaining strips.

5 Place the triangles on a nonstick cookie sheet and lightly mist with oil. Bake in a preheated oven at 400° for 15-20 minutes, until golden.

6 Serve warm or at room temperature with crisp chunks of fresh vegetables and a bowl of nonfat plain yogurt mixed with some toasted cumin seeds and chopped fresh mint.

NUTRITIONAL ANALYSIS

(figures are per parcel)

Calories = 37
Fat = 0.9g
of which saturates = 0.3g
     monounsaturates = 0.3g
     polyunsaturates = 0.1g
Protein = 3.8g
Carbohydrate = 3.8g
Dietary fiber = 0.4g
Sodium = 0.01g

Percentage of total calories from fat = 21%
of which saturates = 7%
Good source of B vitamins

PORK
PITA POCKETS

Pita pockets stuffed with spicy morsels of ground broiled pork and crisp salad make a healthy, well-balanced snack or addition to a lunch box.

Preparation time: 25 minutes, plus chilling

Cooking time: 15 minutes

Serves 4

$^1/_4$ cup minced onion
6 tbsp minced flat-leafed parsley
1 cup extra-lean ground pork
2 tbsp fresh bread crumbs
$^1/_4$ tsp ground cumin
pinch of cayenne
salt and freshly ground black pepper
2 tbsp nonfat plain yogurt

To Serve
2 large pita breads
shredded lettuce
sliced tomatoes and cucumber
lemon wedges
nonfat plain yogurt

1 Place the onion and parsley in a blender and process until very finely minced.

2 Combine the pork, bread crumbs, cumin, cayenne, and salt and pepper in a mixing bowl. Add the onion-and-parsley mixture, mixing until evenly blended, then add the yogurt.

3 Form the mixture into 12 small cylindrical patties. Cover and chill for 1 hour. Thread onto 4 skewers.

4 Preheat the broiler until very hot. Broil for 15 minutes, turning, until brown and cooked through.

5 Cut the pita breads in half crosswise. Fill with salad, the grilled patties, and a lemon wedge. Top with a spoonful of yogurt.

VARIATION
● Replace the pork with ground turkey or chicken.

NUTRITIONAL ANALYSIS

(figures are per serving)

Calories = 88
Fat = 2.5g
of which saturates = 0.8g
     monounsaturates = 0.9g
     polyunsaturates = 0.4g
Protein = 13.0g
Carbohydrate = 3.6g
Dietary fiber = 0.9g
Sodium = 0.06g

Percentage of total calories from fat = 26%
of which saturates = 8%
Good source of B vitamins, iron, & zinc

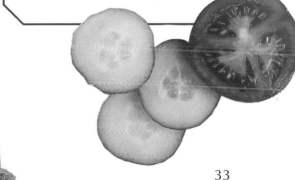

TURKEY STIR-FRY
WITH BOK CHOY & NOODLES

Serve this as a light lunch or supper.

Preparation time: 20 minutes
Cooking time: 15 minutes
Serves 4

8 ounces thin rice noodles
1 tsp peanut oil
3 tbsp Fat-Free Chicken Broth (page 16)
2 garlic cloves, crushed
1-inch piece fresh root ginger, minced
2 fresh red chilies, seeded and very thinly sliced
1 pound turkey breast, cut into thin strips
3 green onions (scallions), sliced into 1-inch diagonal pieces
1 cup thinly sliced brown mushrooms
1 pound 5 ounces bok choy, chopped
1 tbsp light soy sauce
2 tbsp chopped fresh coriander (cilantro)
salt and freshly ground black pepper

NUTRITIONAL ANALYSIS

(figures are per serving)

Calories = 372
Fat = 2.2g
of which saturates = 0.6g
       monounsaturates = 0.7g
       polyunsaturates = 0.6g
Protein = 34.7g
Carbohydrate = 52.1g
Dietary fiber = 1.0g
Sodium = 0.55g

Percentage of total calories from fat = 5%
of which saturates = 1%
Good source of vitamins A, C, & B vitamins, iron, & zinc

1 Cook the noodles according to the instructions on the package. Rinse under a cold running faucet for a few seconds, then leave to drain and cool.

2 Heat a wok or large skillet over medium-high heat. When it is hot, add the oil and broth. Add the garlic, ginger, and chilies, and stir-fry for a few seconds.

3 Add the turkey and stir-fry for 2 minutes until no longer pink. Then add the onions, mushrooms, and soy sauce, and stir-fry for 2 minutes. Add the bok choy and stir-fry for another 2 minutes. Add the coriander (cilantro) and season to taste with salt and pepper.

4 Stir in the noodles until heated through. Serve the stir-fry immediately by itself or with steamed rice.

VARIATION
● If bok choy is unavailable, use Swiss chard or spinach instead.

RED ONION
MARMALADE

Preparation time: 10 minutes
Cooking time: 55 minutes
Makes ²/₃ cup

1 pound red onions, thinly sliced
4 tbsp Fat-Free Chicken Broth (page 16) or Strong Vegetable Broth (page 16)
1 tbsp red wine vinegar
2 tsp olive oil
1 bay leaf, broken into pieces
freshly ground black pepper

1 Place the onion slices in a bowl and toss with the remaining ingredients.

2 Transfer the onion mixture to a large heavy-based nonstick skillet. Cover and cook over medium heat for 5 minutes, stirring occasionally, until the onions are translucent.

3 Reduce the heat to very low, then continue to cook, covered, for 45 minutes until very soft, stirring occasionally. Remove the lid and cook for a further 5 minutes, until very soft and thick.

4 Serve hot or cold with broiled meats, poultry, or fish.

LEMON & MINT
TURKEY BURGERS

These almost fat-free burgers are delicious cooked over hot coals. They are ideal for picnics or an informal light meal.

Preparation time: 25 minutes, plus 1 hour chilling

Cooking time: 6 minutes

Serves 4 (makes 8 patties)

1 pound ground turkey
¹/₂ small onion, grated
finely grated rind and juice of 1 small lemon
1 garlic clove, minced
3 tbsp minced fresh mint
pinch of dried red pepper flakes
salt and freshly ground black pepper
2 tbsp lightly beaten egg white
Red Onion Marmalade (see page 34), to serve

1 In a bowl, combine the turkey, onion, lemon rind and juice, garlic, mint, red pepper flakes, and salt and pepper, mixing thoroughly. Stir in the egg white to bind.

2 Shape the mixture into 8 patties about ¹/₂ inch thick. Cover and leave in the refrigerator for at least 1 hour to allow the flavors to develop.

3 Cook in a nonstick ridged skillet for 4-5 minutes each side. Alternatively, cook in a nonstick shallow roasting pan under a very hot broiler.

4 Serve the burgers with red onion marmalade, sesame buns, and a large salad.

VARIATION
● Serve with nonfat plain yogurt mixed with some toasted cumin seeds and chopped fresh mint instead of Red Onion Marmalade.

COOK'S TIP
● Drain off any excess liquid that appears after the burgers have been chilled.

NUTRITIONAL ANALYSIS
(figures are per serving including 2 tbsp Red Onion Marmalade)

Calories = 150
Fat = 1.7g
of which saturates = 0.4g
      monounsaturates = 0.8g
      polyunsaturates = 0.3g
Protein = 29.1g
Carbohydrate = 5.0g
Dietary fiber = 0.9g
Sodium = 0.08g

Percentage of total calories from fat = 35%
of which saturates = 6%
Good source of B vitamins & zinc

CHICKEN & VEGETABLE
STIR-FRY

Serve this as a light lunch or supper dish.

Preparation time: 20 minutes

Cooking time: 7 minutes

Serves 6

10 ¹/₂ *ounces skinless, boneless chicken breasts, cut
into ³/₄-inch cubes*
salt
4 tsp soy sauce
1 tbsp cornstarch
1 tbsp dry sherry or rice wine
6 tbsp Fat-Free Chicken Broth (page 16)
1 tbsp oyster sauce
4 green onions (scallions)
¹/₂ cup baby corn cobs
¹/₂ cup snow-peas, trimmed
1 cup canned water chestnuts, drained
1 red bell pepper
2 tsp ground nut oil
³/₄-inch piece fresh ginger root, minced
2 garlic cloves, minced
1 tsp dark sesame oil
1¹/₄ tsp sesame seeds

1 Place the chicken in a bowl with
¹/₄ tsp salt, 2 tsp of the soy sauce, the
cornstarch, and sherry, stirring to coat.
Leave to stand for 15 minutes.

2 Mix the remaining soy sauce with the
broth and oyster sauce, and set aside.

3 Diagonally slice the green onions
(scallions) into ³/₄-inch pieces. Cut the
corn into 3 pieces. Diagonally slice the
snow-peas into halves. Halve the water
chestnuts horizontally and cut the bell
pepper into similar sized pieces.

4 Place a nonstick wok or large skillet
over medium-high heat. When the pan is
hot, add the peanut oil. When it sizzles,
add the ginger, garlic, and green onions
(scallions). Stir quickly, then add the
onions, corn, water chestnuts, and bell
pepper. Stir-fry for 2 minutes. Sprinkle
with the sesame oil and a little salt.

5 Add the chicken and stir-fry for
3 minutes until it is no longer pink.

6 Add the snow-peas and the soy sauce
mixture. Stir-fry for 1 minute, until
thickened. Sprinkle with sesame seeds
and serve at once. Serve with plainly
cooked rice.

VARIATION
● Use broccoli flowerets in place
of the corn.

COOK'S TIP
● The secret of a successful stir-fry
is to cook over high heat for
the minimum amount of time.
You need to have all the
ingredients prepared
and to hand before
you begin.

CHICKEN TERIYAKI

In this dish, the chicken breasts are richly glazed with honey and soy sauce. Serve as a light lunch or supper.

Preparation time: 20 minutes, plus marinating

Cooking time: 10 minutes

Serves 6

NUTRITIONAL ANALYSIS

(figures are per serving)

Calories = 101
Fat = 1.4g
of which saturates = 0.3g
    monounsaturates = 0.5g
    polyunsaturates = 0.4g
Protein = 13.7g
Carbohydrate = 8.2g
Dietary fiber = 1.3g
Sodium = 0.34g

Percentage of total calories from fat = 12%
of which saturates = 2%
Good source of vitamin A & B vitamins

6 skinless, boneless chicken breasts, weighing about 4 ounces each
vegetable oil spray

FOR THE MARINADE
3 tbsp clear honey
¹/₂ cup tamari (Japanese soy sauce)
¹/₂ cup dry sherry
1-inch piece fresh ginger root, minced
1 garlic clove, crushed
¹/₂ tsp freshly ground black pepper
lemon wedges and sprigs of flat-leafed parsley, to garnish

1 Cut the chicken breasts in half diagonally and place in a bowl.

2 Place the marinade ingredients in a small saucepan and bring to the boil. Allow to cool, then pour the marinade over the chicken. Leave to marinate for at least 2 hours or overnight, turning occasionally.

3 Remove the chicken from the marinade and shake off the excess liquid. Reserve the marinade.

4 Lightly spray with oil a nonstick skillet large enough to take the chicken breasts in a single layer. Place over medium-high heat until hot, then add the chicken. Fry for 2-3 minutes until browned on both sides.

5 Add the reserved marinade. Bring to the boil, then reduce the heat slightly, and simmer briskly for 5 minutes.

6 Transfer the chicken breasts to a heated serving dish. Reduce the liquid remaining in the pan over a high heat and pour it over the chicken. Garnish with lemon wedges and sprigs of parsley.

7 Serve the chicken with boiled rice and a stir-fried leafy vegetable.

NUTRITIONAL ANALYSIS

(figures are per serving)

Calories = 158
Fat = 1.3g
of which saturates = 0.4g
    monounsaturates = 0.6g
    polyunsaturates = 0.2g

Protein = 29.4g
Carbohydrate = 2.2g
Dietary fiber = 0.00g
Sodium = 1.17g

Percentage of total calories from fat = 7%
of which saturates = 2%
Good source of B vitamins

CHICKEN BREASTS
WITH VERMOUTH &
WATERCRESS SAUCE

*This quickly cooked entrée
would be ideal for a dinner party.*

Preparation time: 15 minutes
Cooking time: 25 minutes
Serves 4

*4 skinless, boneless chicken breasts, weighing
about 6 ounces each
freshly ground black pepper
²⁄₃ cup Fat-Free Chicken Broth (page 16)
2 shallots, minced
4 tbsp dry vermouth
1 bunch trimmed watercress, chopped
salt
2 tsp arrowroot, mixed with 1 tbsp orange juice or
cold water
orange segments, to garnish*

1 Cut the chicken breasts in half
diagonally. Season with plenty of coarsely
ground black pepper.

2 Fry the chicken in a heavy-based
nonstick skillet for 2-3 minutes each
side, to seal. Remove from the pan and
set aside.

3 Add 2 tbsp of the broth and the
shallots to the pan. Wet-fry for 2 minutes
until soft.

4 Add the vermouth and remaining
broth to the pan. Bring to the boil
and add the chicken. Reduce the heat,
cover, and simmer over low heat
for 15-20 minutes.

5 Stir in the watercress and season to
taste with salt and pepper.

6 Raise the heat, add the arrowroot, and
stir for 1 minute until thickened.

7 Transfer to a heated serving dish and
pour the sauce over the chicken. Garnish
with orange segments and serve with
steamed new potatoes and carrots cut
into matchstick strips.

VARIATIONS
● Use turkey
breast instead of
chicken.
● Replace the
watercress with
3 tbsp of chopped fresh
herbs such as tarragon
or basil.

COOK'S TIP
● Vermouth is a fortified wine,
enriched with herbs and spices,
which makes an aromatic basis for a
sauce. If you do not have any, use dry
white wine instead.

NUTRITIONAL ANALYSIS
(figures are per serving)

Calories = 214
Fat = 2.1g
of which saturates = 0.6g
      monounsaturates = 0.9g
      polyunsaturates = 0.4g
Protein = 42.5g
Carbohydrate = 3.5g
Dietary fiber = 0.5g
Sodium = 0.11g

Percentage of total calories from fat = 9%,
of which saturates = 2%
Good source of B vitamins, iron, & zinc

BROILED POUSSINS

With the skin removed, these spicy poussins make a delicious low-fat entrée.
Alternatively, use rock Cornish game hens instead of the poussins.

Preparation time: 30 minutes, plus marinating

Cooking time: 25 minutes

Serves 4

2 poussins or rock Cornish game
hens, weighing about 14 ounces each
1 tbsp lemon juice
1$^1/_4$ tsp salt
$^1/_4$ tsp freshly ground black pepper
$^1/_4$ tsp cayenne pepper
6 tbsp nonfat plain yogurt
1-inch piece fresh root ginger, minced
$^1/_2$ small onion, grated
3 garlic cloves, crushed
1 tbsp coriander (cilantro) seeds,
toasted and crushed
vegetable oil spray

1 Place the poussins or rock Cornish game hens on a board, breast side downward. Using poultry shears or strong kitchen scissors, cut along the entire length of either side of the backbone. Discard the backbone, pope's nose, and leg and wing tips.

2 Halve the birds lengthwise by cutting through the breastbone. Remove the skin. Make parallel cuts through the thick part of the breast and thighs, almost to the bone.

3 Combine the lemon juice, salt, black pepper, and cayenne pepper. Rub the mixture over the poussins and into the flesh. Set aside for 30 minutes.

4 Combine the yogurt, ginger, onion, garlic, and coriander (cilantro) seeds. Add to the poussins, turning to coat and rubbing the mixture into the flesh. Cover and leave to marinate in the refrigerator for at least 4 hours or overnight.

5 Thread the poussin halves onto 4 skewers, pushing the skewer lengthwise through the leg and the wing.

6 Preheat the broiler until very hot. Place the poussins skin side upward on a rack in a broiler pan. Lightly spray with oil from a spray can. Position the pan 6 inches from the heat source. Broil for 15 minutes, then turn over and broil for a further 10 minutes, until the juices run clear when a skewer is inserted into the thigh.

7 Transfer to a warmed serving platter and serve with lime wedges, shredded lettuce, sliced tomatoes, onion rings, pita bread, and a bowl of nonfat yogurt.

NUTRITIONAL ANALYSIS

(figures are per serving)

Calories = 195
Fat = 2.5g
of which saturates = 0.5g
     monounsaturates = 1.1g
     polyunsaturates = 0.5g

Protein = 41.0g
Carbohydrate = 3.0g
Dietary fiber = 0.2g
Sodium = 0.1g

Percentage of total calories from fat = 11%, of which saturates = 3%
Good source of B vitamins

PORK STEAKS WITH
KUMQUAT SAUCE

*This low-fat entrée would be ideal to serve for a winter dinner party,
when kumquats are available.*

Preparation time: 20 minutes

Cooking time: 45 minutes

Serves 4

³/₄ cup kumquats, quartered lengthwise
1 tsp coriander (cilantro) seeds, toasted and crushed
1²/₃ cups Fat-Free Chicken Broth (page 16)
*4 pork steaks, trimmed of fat, weighing
about 5 ounces each*
freshly ground black pepper
2 shallots, minced
1 tbsp chopped fresh rosemary
1 tsp sugar
2 tsp red wine vinegar
salt
small sprigs of rosemary, to garnish

1 Place the kumquats in a saucepan with
the coriander (cilantro) seeds and 1¼ cups
of the broth. Bring to the boil, cover, and
simmer gently for 20 minutes. Set aside.

2 Season the steaks with pepper. Dry-fry
in a heavy-based nonstick skillet over
medium-high heat for 1 minute on each
side. Remove from the pan and set aside.

3 Reduce the heat and add the
remaining broth to the pan with the

shallots and rosemary. Wet-fry for
2 minutes, until the shallots are soft.

4 Pour the kumquat mixture into the pan
and stir in the sugar and vinegar. Add the
steaks and bring to the boil. Reduce the
heat, then cover and simmer over low heat
for 20 minutes, until the pork is tender.

5 Check the seasoning, then transfer to a
warmed serving platter. Garnish with the
rosemary and serve with
boiled potatoes and
steamed green vegetables.

VARIATION
● Use fresh cranberries in
place of the kumquats. If
you do, omit the vinegar
and add extra sugar to taste.

COOK'S TIP
● Kumquats cook down to a
refreshingly sharp sauce
which contrasts well with
the richness of pork.

NUTRITIONAL ANALYSIS

(figures are per serving)

Calories = 188

Fat = 3.7g

of which saturates = 1.1g

    monounsaturates = 1.4g

    polyunsaturates = 0.6g

Protein = 33.1g

Carbohydrate = 6.0g

Dietary fiber = 0.1g

Sodium = 0.1g

Percentage of total calories from fat = 18%, of which saturates = 5%

Good source of B vitamins, iron, & zinc

PORK & PEPPER
KABOBS

Serve these spicy kabobs as a entrée.
They are delicious cooked on the barbecue.

Preparation time: 20 minutes, plus marinating

Cooking time: 15 minutes

Serves 4

6 tbsp nonfat plain yogurt
1 tsp cumin seeds, toasted and crushed
1 tsp coriander (cilantro) seeds,
toasted and crushed
$^1/_4$-$^1/_2$ tsp harissa sauce
juice of 1 lime
sea salt and freshly ground black pepper
10$^1/_2$ ounces extra lean pork,
cut into $^3/_4$-inch cubes
1 green bell pepper, seeded and
cut into $^3/_4$-inch squares
olive oil spray
4 bay leaves, broken in half

1 Combine the yogurt, cumin, and coriander (cilantro) seeds, hot pepper sauce, lime juice, salt, and pepper.

2 Place the meat in a bowl with the yogurt mixture and toss to coat.

Cover and marinate in the refrigerator for at least 4 hours or overnight.

3 Lightly spray the bell pepper pieces with olive oil from a spray can.

4 Thread the meat, bell peppers, and bay leaves onto 4 skewers. Lightly spray with olive oil.

5 Place under a preheated very hot broiler, and cook for 12-15 minutes, turning frequently until browned.

6 Serve the kabobs with steamed rice, a bowl of low-fat yogurt, and a salad.

COOK'S TIP
● Harissa sauce is a very hot sauce from North Africa, sold in tubes or small cans. The hot pepper sauces from Louisiana are very similar in flavor.

NUTRITIONAL ANALYSIS

(figures are per serving)

Calories = 114
Fat = 4.1g
of which saturates = 1.2g
monounsaturates = 1.9g
polyunsaturates = 0.7g

Protein = 17.4g
Carbohydrate = 2.4g
Dietary fiber = 0.7g
Sodium = 0.06g

Percentage of total calories from fat = 33 %, of which saturates = 9%
Good source of B vitamins & vitamin C

LAMB, EGGPLANT, & CHICK-PEA
CASSEROLE

*Even lean lamb contains hidden fat, so this recipe contains a relatively
small amount of meat but plenty of carbohydrate-rich chick-peas and pita
bread. It is ideal for a comforting winter dinner.*

Preparation time: 40 minutes, plus soaking and cooking the chick-peas

Cooking time: 1 hour 40 minutes

Serves 6

1 cup chick-peas (garbanzo beans),
soaked overnight
1 eggplant, cut into ³/₄-inch slices
¹/₄ tsp ground cinnamon
large pinch of cayenne
large pinch of ground allspice
freshly ground black pepper
8 ounces extra-lean lamb, cut into ³/₄-inch cubes
1 large onion, chopped
1¹/₂ cups Fat-Free Meat Broth (page 17)
1 large red bell pepper, cut into ³/₄-inch squares
14-ounce can peeled, chopped tomatoes
finely grated rind of 1 lemon
salt
1 large pita bread, opened flat and toasted
¹/₃ cup nonfat plain yogurt
2 tbsp chopped fresh mint
1 garlic clove, crushed
toasted cumin seeds, to garnish

1 Drain the chick-peas (garbanzo beans),
place in a saucepan with fresh water, and
bring to the boil. Simmer briskly until
just tender, then drain.

2 Arrange the eggplant slices in a single
layer in a nonstick broiler pan. Broil for
10-12 minutes, turning once, until
golden. Cut into bite-sized segments.

3 Rub the cinnamon, cayenne, allspice,
and a little black pepper into the meat.

4 Place the onion and 2 tbsp of the broth
in a nonstick skillet over medium heat.
Wet-fry for 4-5 minutes, until
translucent. Add the meat and sauté for
5 minutes, until browned.

5 Transfer the meat and onions to a
heavy-based casserole. Add the bell

pepper, eggplants, chick-peas (garbanzo
beans), tomatoes, and remaining broth.
Add the lemon rind and season with salt
and pepper. Bring to the boil, then cover
and simmer for 1-1¹/₄ hours until the
lamb is tender.

6 Break the pita bread into pieces and
spread it over the base of a shallow
dish. Drain the meat and
vegetables, reserving the
liquid, and arrange
over the bread.
Spoon over a

little of the liquid and pour the
remainder into a sauceboat.

7 Mix the yogurt with the mint, garlic,
and a little salt. Spoon this over the
lamb, sprinkle with cumin seeds, and
serve immediately with a salad.

VENISON CHILI

Being naturally very lean, venison makes a healthy alternative to beef.
Buffalo could be used instead.

Preparation time: 30 minutes, plus soaking beans

Cooking time: 1 hour 50 minutes

Serves 8

1 cup black turtle beans, soaked overnight
¹/₂ cup navy beans, soaked overnight
2 tsp cumin seeds
2 tsp coriander (cilantro) seeds
2 tsp dried oregano
1 tsp olive oil
2-3 cups Fat-Free Meat Broth (page 17)
3 pounds boneless venison, cubed
2 onions, chopped
3 garlic cloves, minced
2 red bell peppers, cored, seeded, and
cut into ³/₄-inch squares
2-3 tsp chili powder, or to taste
2 x 14-ounce cans peeled, chopped tomatoes
3 tbsp tomato paste
1 tsp sugar
1 tsp salt
6 tbsp chopped fresh coriander (cilantro)

1 Drain the beans, place in separate saucepans, and cover with fresh water. Boil rapidly for 15 minutes, then simmer until just tender. Drain and set aside.

2 Dry-fry the seeds over medium heat until fragrant. Add the oregano and fry for a few seconds more. Remove from the pan and lightly crush with a pestle in a mortar.

3 Fry the venison in a nonstick skillet, in batches if necessary, over medium-high heat for 15 minutes until browned and any moisture has evaporated. Sprinkle with half the toasted spices and fry for a few minutes more. Transfer to a casserole.

4 Add the oil and 4 tbsp of the broth to the skillet. Wet-fry the onion, garlic, bell pepper, chili, and remaining toasted spices over medium heat for 5 minutes, until the onion is soft.

5 Add the mixture to the meat, together with the tomatoes, tomato paste, sugar, salt, beans, and about 2 cups of the broth. Bring to the boil, then cover and simmer for 45 minutes, stirring occasionally.

6 Stir in the coriander (cilantro) and simmer for a further 5 minutes. Serve with boiled rice or warm tortillas and a green side salad.

NUTRITIONAL ANALYSIS

(figures are per serving)

Calories = 233
Fat = 5.0g
of which saturates = 0.3g
     monounsaturates = 0.4g
     polyunsaturates = 1.1g
Protein = 18.4g
Carbohydrate = 30.2g
Dietary fiber = 5.1g
Sodium = 0.11g

Percentage of total calories from fat = 20%
of which saturates = 1%
Good source of B vitamins, iron, & zinc

NUTRITIONAL ANALYSIS

(figures are per serving)

Calories = 333
Fat = 4.6g
of which saturates = 1.6g
     monounsaturates = 1.4g
     polyunsaturates = 1.1g

Protein = 47.5g
Carbohydrate = 28.4g
Dietary fiber = 4.7g
Sodium = 0.15g

Percentage of total calories from fat = 13%, of which saturates = 4%
Good source of vitamins A, C, & B vitamins, iron, & zinc

CHAPTER THREE

FISH & SEAFOOD

Packed with protein, vitamins, and minerals and containing very little fat, fish and seafood are among the most nutritious foods available. The fat found in all fish is mainly of the unsaturated type and contains essential fatty acids which are important for health. However, the amount of fat present varies depending on the type of fish, and even the season of the year. White fish are lowest in fat — monkfish, cod, red snapper, and porgy (sea-bream) contain less than 1%. Seafood is also low in fat but it does contain cholesterol. Oily fish such as salmon, trout, and tuna contain 5-20 % fat, which makes these varieties difficult to include in a virtually fat-free diet, unless you eat them in very small quantities.

MUSSEL & POTATO
SOUP

Packed with robust flavors, this soup is a meal in itself. Serve it for lunch with plenty of salad and freshly baked bread.

Preparation time: 50 minutes

Cooking time: 50 minutes

Serves 4

3¹/₂ pounds mussels, cleaned and bearded
1 quart water
1 onion, minced
4 garlic cloves, minced
3 parsley sprigs
3 rosemary sprigs
1 bay leaf
¹/₄ tsp black peppercorns
1 cup sliced waxy new potatoes
2 plum tomatoes, seeded and finely diced
salt
chopped flat-leafed parsley, to garnish

1 Place the mussels in a large heavy-based saucepan with 1 cup of the water. Cook, tightly covered, over high heat for 5 minutes, until the shells open, shaking the pan occasionally.

2 Strain the cooking liquid through a sieve lined with cheesecloth and reserve it. Discard any mussels that have not opened. Set aside a few mussels for

garnish. Remove the rest from their shells and reserve them.

3 Place the remaining water in a saucepan with the garlic, parsley, rosemary, bay leaf, and peppercorns. Bring to the boil, then simmer, partially covered, for 30 minutes.

4 Strain the garlic-and-herb infusion and mix with the mussel cooking liquid. Return the liquid to the pan and add the potatoes. Simmer for 15 minutes, until the potatoes are cooked.

5 Add the diced tomatoes and the mussels, including those in their shells. Simmer until the mussels are heated through.

6 Ladle the soup into warmed bowls, making sure each serving gets a few mussels in their shells. Garnish with parsley.

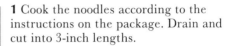

ORIENTAL
SEAFOOD SOUP

This light but satisfying soup relies on good quality homemade broth. Serve as an appetizer for a Chinese meal.

Preparation time: 15 minutes

Cooking time: 20 minutes

Serves 4

NUTRITIONAL ANALYSIS

(figures are per serving)

Calories = 246

Fat — 4.9g

of which saturates = 1.1g

      monounsaturates = 0.8g

      polyunsaturates = 1.7g

Protein = 32.0g

Carbohydrate = 19.7g

Dietary fiber = 1.9g

Sodium = 0.73g

Percentage of total calories from fat = 18%

of which saturates = 4%

Good source of potassium, iron, zinc, & B vitamins

2 ounces thin rice noodles
3 cups Fat-Free Chicken Broth (page 16)
2 stalks lemon grass, crushed
2 tsp ginger juice
6 green onions (scallions), thinly sliced
salt
12 ounces cod, skinned and cut into chunks
¹/₃ cup thinly sliced mushrooms
1 small green chili, seeded and thinly sliced
¹/₃ cup corn kernels
2 tsp fish sauce
pinch of sugar
2 tbsp lime juice
2 tbsp chopped fresh coriander
(cilantro)

1 Cook the noodles according to the instructions on the package. Drain and cut into 3-inch lengths.

2 Place the broth, lemon grass, ginger juice, and green onions (scallions) into a saucepan. Bring to the boil and season with salt.

3 Add the fish, mushrooms, and chili. Simmer gently for 10 minutes until the fish is nearly cooked, then add the corn and cook for another 2 minutes.

4 Stir in the noodles, fish sauce, sugar, and lime juice. Simmer for another minute. Sprinkle with coriander (cilantro) and serve.

VARIATIONS
● Add a few bay shrimp to the fish.
● Use garden peas instead of corn.

NUTRITIONAL ANALYSIS

(figures are per serving)

Calories = 198

Fat = 1.1g

of which saturates = 0.2g

      monounsaturates = 0.2g

      polyunsaturates = 0.4g

Protein = 18.7g

Carbohydrate = 27.6g

Dietary fiber = 0.9g

Sodium = 0.06g

Percentage of total calories from fat = 5%

of which saturates = 0.7%

Good source of potassium & B vitamins

SMOKED SALMON
SALAD

*This colorful salad is full of contrasting flavors and textures —
rich, velvety smoked salmon, juicy pink grapefruit, peppery watercress,
crunchy radishes, and crisp celery. Serve it as a tasty appetizer
or with a bowl of soup as a light lunch.*

Preparation time: 20 minutes
Serves 2

NUTRITIONAL ANALYSIS
(figures are per serving)

Calories = 253
Fat = 4.1g
of which saturates = 0.9g
      monounsaturates = 1.1g
      polyunsaturates = 0.7g
Protein = 20.9g
Carbohydrate = 35.4g
Dietary fiber = 7.5g
Sodium = 1.06g

Percentage of total calories from fat = 15%, of
which saturates = 3%
Good source of calcium, potassium, iron, & B
vitamins

1 pink grapefruit
$^1/_2$ cup low-fat small curd cottage cheese
*2 tbsp chopped fresh herbs, such as
dill, chives, or sorrel*
salt and freshly ground black pepper
$^1/_2$ head radicchio, torn into bite-sized pieces
handful of small lettuce leaves
handful of watercress, trimmed
olive oil spray
*2 slices (about 2 ounces) smoked salmon (lox),
cut into strips*
4 radishes, sliced
2 small celery stalks, diagonally sliced
2 slices of whole-grain rye bread, to serve

1 Using a very sharp knife, cut a
horizontal slice from the top and bottom
of the grapefruit, exposing the flesh.
Remove the remaining peel and all the
white parts by cutting downward,
following the contours of the fruit.

2 Working over a bowl to catch the
juices, cut down between the flesh and
membrane of each segment and ease out
the flesh. Add the segments to the juice
in the bowl.

3 Mix the cottage cheese with the herbs,
salt, and pepper to taste.

4 Lightly spray the radicchio, lettuce,
and watercress with oil from a spray, and
sprinkle with a tablespoon of the
grapefruit juice. Season with freshly
ground pepper and a pinch of salt.

5 Arrange the leaves and watercress on
individual plates. Scatter with the
smoked salmon (lox), radishes, celery,
and half the grapefruit segments (use

the remainder in a fruit salad). Add a
small mound of the cottage cheese
mixture and serve with the rye bread.

VARIATIONS
● Use arugula instead of watercress.
● Replace the celery with asparagus.

CEVICHE
OF SOLE

Raw fish is "cooked" in citrus juice in this colorful appetizer or entrée salad.

Preparation time: 35 minutes

Cooking time: 25 minutes

Serves 4

*14 ounces sole, flounder,
or dab, skinned
juice of 2 oranges
juice of 2 limes
1/2 small red onion, minced
3 small green chilies,
seeded and finely diced
3 garlic cloves, peeled and minced
salt
freshly ground black pepper
1 medium sweet potato, unpeeled
6 tomatoes, puréed and sieved
2 tbsp sherry
4 handfuls crisp lettuce, such
as iceberg or romaine
1/2 green bell pepper, seeded
and finely diced
6 shelled cooked jumbo shrimp
3 tbsp chopped fresh coriander (cilantro)*

1 Cut the fish into very thin strips and place in a non acid-reactive bowl.

2 Combine the orange and lime juice, onion, chilies, garlic, salt, and pepper. Pour the mixture over the fish and leave to marinate in the refrigerator for 3-4 hours. The fish will turn opaque and virtually cook.

3 Steam the sweet potato for 15-20 minutes, until just tender. Allow to cool, then remove the peel. Dice the flesh finely and set aside.

4 Remove the fish from the marinade, scraping back into the marinade as many of the diced vegetables as possible. Cover the fish and refrigerate. Pour the marinade into a small saucepan.

5 Add the puréed tomato and the sherry. Bring to the boil, then simmer briskly for about 5 minutes, until reduced. Leave to cool then check the seasoning, adding more salt and pepper if necessary.

6 Arrange the lettuce leaves on individual plates with the fish on top. Scatter the sweet potato and bell pepper over the top, then add the jumbo shrimp. Spoon over the sauce, and sprinkle with the coriander (cilantro). Serve with crusty bread.

NUTRITIONAL ANALYSIS

(figures are per serving)

Calories = 220
Fat = 2.7g
of which saturates = 0.5g
      monounsaturates = 0.5g
      polyunsaturates = 1.1g
Protein = 27.0g
Carbohydrate = 21.6g
Dietary fiber = 4.2g
Sodium = 0.21g

Percentage of total calories from fat = 11%
of which saturates = 2%
Good source of potassium, iron, zinc, vitamins A, E, & B vitamins

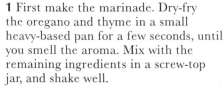

SHRIMP & MONKFISH
KABOBS

*Cooked over hot coals or under the broiler, these succulent
kabobs make a light and tasty dinner.*

Preparation time: 30 minutes, plus marinating

Cooking time: 10 minutes

Serves 4

FOR THE MARINADE

¹/₂ tsp dried oregano
¹/₂ tsp dried thyme
5 tbsp lemon juice
finely grated rind of ¹/₂ lemon
1 tbsp olive oil
1 garlic clove, crushed
salt and freshly ground black pepper

8 jumbo shrimp, unshelled
8 ounces monkfish fillets, cut into 1-inch cubes
*¹/₂ yellow and ¹/₂ green bell pepper, cut into 1-inch
squares*
1 red onion, cut into 1-inch chunks
¹/₃ cup button mushrooms
lettuce, to serve

1 First make the marinade. Dry-fry the oregano and thyme in a small heavy-based pan for a few seconds, until you smell the aroma. Mix with the remaining ingredients in a screw-top jar, and shake well.

2 Shell the shrimp, but leave the tail intact.

3 Place the shrimp and monkfish in a shallow dish, and the vegetables in another. Divide the marinade between each dish, turning the fish and vegetables until coated. Cover and leave in the refrigerator for at least 2 hours.

4 Thread the ingredients onto 4 skewers, alternating the monkfish and shrimp with the vegetables.

5 Cook over hot coals, or under a preheated hot broiler, for 10 minutes, turning occasionally.

6 Arrange the lettuce in a shallow serving dish and place the kabobs on top.

7 Serve with warm pita bread and a bowl of nonfat yogurt seasoned with chopped fresh mint, salt, and cayenne pepper.

NUTRITIONAL ANALYSIS

(figures are per serving)

Calories = 107
Fat = 3.4g
of which saturates = 0.5g
      monounsaturates = 2.1g
      polyunsaturates = 0.5g
Protein = 14.8g
Carbohydrate = 4.6g
Dietary fiber = 1.4g
Sodium = 0.07g

Percentage of total calories from fat = 29%
of which saturates = 5%
Good source of potassium, iron, & B vitamins

BROILED CALAMARI
WITH TOMATO & LENTIL SALSA

Charbroiled calamari makes an excellent appetizer or light meal.

Preparation time: 35 minutes, plus marinating

Cooking time: 15 minutes

Serves 4

FOR THE SALSA
¹/₂ cup small brown lentils
juice of 2 limes
1 tsp grated orange rind
2 tsp olive oil
salt and freshly ground black pepper
¹/₂ cup finely diced fennel
3 firm tomatoes, seeded and finely diced
2 green onions (scallions),
green parts included, minced
3 tbsp chopped fresh fennel leaves
1 tbsp chopped or flat leafed parsley

1 pound 5 ounces calamari (squid)
olive oil spray
salt
freshly ground black pepper
2 large handfuls of frisée or escarole
lime wedges, to garnish

1 To make the salsa, place the lentils in a saucepan, cover with water, and bring to the boil. Cover and simmer for 12-15 minutes, or until the lentils are just tender but with some bite.

2 Drain off any liquid from the lentils. While they are still warm, toss with the lime juice, orange rind, olive oil, and plenty of sea salt and coarsely ground black pepper. Allow to cool a little, then mix in the rest of the salsa ingredients. Leave to stand at room temperature for at least 1 hour.

3 Clean the squid, removing the beak and the inner quill, and discard the tentacles. Rinse in cold water, drain, and pat dry. Cut the fins from the pouch and reserve. Cut the pouch into 3-inch triangles. Lightly spray the triangles and fins with oil and season generously with salt and pepper.

4 Heat a ridged nonstick skillet or griddle until very hot. Place the squid pieces on it, and broil for about 30 seconds or until they start to curl. Turn over and broil the other side for another 30 seconds. Immediately remove from the broiler.

5 Arrange the frisée or escarole on individual plates. Add the squid, garnish with lime wedges, and serve with the salsa.

NUTRITIONAL ANALYSIS

(figures are per serving)

Calories = 191

Fat = 4.4g

of which saturates = 0.8g

    monounsaturates = 1.6g

    polyunsaturates = 1.1g

Protein = 23.7g

Carbohydrate = 15.3g

Dietary fiber = 1.1g

Sodium = 0.14g

Percentage of total calories from fat = 21%, of which saturates = 4%

Good source of potassium, iron, zinc, B vitamins, & vitamin E

HALIBUT STEAKS
PROVENÇAL

Meaty halibut and a broiled tomato sauce topped with diced peppers, zucchini, and eggplant make a richly flavored but low-fat main meal.

Preparation time: 35 minutes

Cooking time: 35 minutes

Serves 4

NUTRITIONAL ANALYSIS
(figures are per serving)

Calories = 217
Fat = 3.9g
of which saturates = 0.7g
       monounsaturates = 1.22g
       polyunsaturates = 1.11g
Protein = 34.7g
Carbohydrate = 11.3g
Dietary fiber = 3.5g
Sodium = 0.35g

Percentage of total calories from fat = 16%
of which saturates = 3%
Good source of potassium, iron,
vitamins A, E, & B vitamins

FOR THE SAUCE
1¼ pounds plum tomatoes
4 large garlic cloves, unpeeled
1 red bell pepper, halved and seeded
2 tsp dried oregano
2 tbsp Fat-Free Chicken Broth (page 16)
½ onion, minced
2 tsp wine vinegar
½ tsp sugar
½ tsp salt
freshly ground black pepper

4 halibut steaks, weighing about 6 ounces each
salt and freshly ground black pepper
flour, for dusting
olive oil spray
5 tbsp Fat-free Chicken Broth (page 16)
¼ cup each of finely diced zucchini, eggplant, and red and yellow bell peppers

1 First make the sauce. Place the tomatoes, garlic, and bell peppers in a roasting pan, allowing plenty of space between them. Roast in a preheated oven at 450°, until the skins blacken and blister. The garlic will need about 10 minutes, and the tomatoes and bell pepper 20 minutes.

2 Peel the garlic and bell pepper, but leave the tomatoes unpeeled.

3 Dry-fry the oregano in a small heavy-based pan until you can smell the aroma.

4 Heat the broth in another small pan. Wet-fry the onion until translucent. Add the vinegar and oregano and cook for another minute.

5 Purée the tomatoes, garlic, and bell peppers with the onion mixture until smooth. Press through a sieve, then pour into a small saucepan. Add the sugar, and salt and pepper to taste. Reheat gently and keep warm.

6 Season the fish well and dust with flour. Lightly spray a nonstick skillet with oil, and place over medium heat. Add the fish, then cover and cook for about 10 minutes, turning frequently, until golden and just cooked through. Remove from the pan and keep warm.

7 Add the broth to the pan over high heat. Add the diced vegetables and cook for 4-5 minutes, or until just tender. Season with salt and pepper.

8 Spoon some of the sauce over 4 warmed plates. Place the fish in the center and add the diced vegetables. Serve with boiled new potatoes.

FLOUNDER FILLETS
WITH MUSHROOM, DILL, & LEMON

These lettuce-wrapped flounder fillets with a light lemony stuffing make an elegant entrée when you have company.

Preparation time: 25 minutes
Cooking time: 15 minutes
Serves 4

8 large crisp lettuce leaves, such as iceberg or romaine
⅓ cup finely diced mushrooms
finely grated rind of 1 large lemon
2 tbsp chopped fresh dill
coarse sea salt
freshly ground black pepper
1 pound flounder fillets, skinned
2 tbsp lemon juice
fresh dill fronds, to garnish

1 Plunge the lettuce leaves into a large pan of boiling salted water for a few seconds. Drain under cold running water. Shave away any thick pieces of stalk and spread out to dry on paper towels.

2 Combine the mushroom, grated lemon rind, and dill with a pinch of sea salt and plenty of freshly ground black pepper.

3 Cut the fillets into 8 pieces and sprinkle with the lemon juice. Place a little of the mushroom mixture on top of each piece and roll up. Wrap each roll in a lettuce leaf, folding over the sides as for a burrito.

4 Place the parcels in a single layer in a steamer basket (cook in batches if necessary).

5 Place the basket over boiling water. Cover and steam for 10 minutes. Remove from the pan and keep warm.

6 Serve, garnished with the dill, with new potatoes and lightly steamed carrot or zucchini strips.

VARIATION
● Use chard or silverbeet leaves instead of lettuce leaves. Remove the ribs and tough stalks.

RED SNAPPER
PARCELS

*Baked in a foil parcel with orange rind and herbs,
red snapper makes an impressive entrée.*

Preparation time: 25 minutes

Cooking time: 30 minutes

Serves 4

1 red snapper, weighing about 2 pounds, cleaned
2 tsp olive oil
salt and freshly ground black pepper
juice and thinly pared rind of ¹/₂ orange
2 tbsp chopped fresh marjoram
2 tbsp chopped fresh thyme
1¹/₂ pounds new potatoes, to serve
orange segments, to garnish

1 Slash the fish on each side with a
sharp knife. Place on a large double
thickness rectangle of aluminum foil.
Brush the oil over the fish, season with
salt and pepper, and sprinkle with the
orange juice.

2 Reserve a tablespoon each of the
marjoram and thyme. Sprinkle the
remainder over both sides of the fish,
stuffing it into the slashed flesh. Cut the
orange rind into thin shreds and scatter
over the fish.

3 Wrap the foil loosely round the fish,
sealing the edges securely to prevent the
juices from escaping.

4 Place on a baking sheet under a preheated hot broiler. Cook for 15 minutes
each side, until cooked through.

5 Transfer to a warmed serving dish.
Sprinkle with the reserved herbs, pour the
cooking juices over the top, and garnish
with orange segments. Serve with the
potatoes and some steamed snow-peas.

NUTRITIONAL ANALYSIS

(figures are per serving, including potatoes)

Calories = 324
Fat = 5.0g
of which saturates = 1.1g
      monounsaturates = 1.6g
      polyunsaturates = 1.2g
Protein = 46.9g
Carbohydrate = 24.5g
Dietary fiber = 2.6g
Sodium = 0.19g

Percentage of total calories
from fat = 14%, of which saturates = 3%
Good source of iron, zinc, selenium,
iodine, & B vitamins

SEAFOOD
RAGOUT

*This hearty Mediterranean-style
fish stew makes an excellent
low-fat entrée.*

Preparation time: 25 minutes

Cooking time: 35 minutes

Serves 6

2 tsp olive oil
1 small onion, chopped
1 small red bell pepper,
seeded and diced
1 small green bell pepper,
seeded and diced
3 garlic cloves, minced
14-ounce can peeled, chopped tomatoes
3 tbsp chopped flat-leafed parsley
1 tbsp tomato paste
²/₃ cup dry red wine
2 thin slices of lemon rind
salt and freshly ground black pepper
12 ounces thick cod steaks, skinned and cubed
6 peeled jumbo shrimp
1 pound fresh mussels, scrubbed and bearded
8 ounces large scallops, sliced

SEARED COD
WITH GREEN CHILI SAUCE

*A brilliant green chili sauce adds fire and color
to this substantial Mexican-style fish dish.*

Preparation time: 25 minutes

Cooking time: 30 minutes

Serves 6

NUTRITIONAL ANALYSIS

(figures are per serving)

Calories = 225
Fat = 3.8g
of which saturates = 0.7g
     monounsaturates = 1.1g
     polyunsaturates = 1.0g
Protein = 35.2g
Carbohydrate = 8.9g
Dietary fiber = 1.8g
Sodium = 0.41g

Percentage of total calories from fat = 15%
of which saturates = 3%
Good source of iron, zinc, iodine,
vitamin A, & B vitamins

FOR THE SAUCE
3-4 tomatillos (green tomatoes)
2 green bell peppers, halved and seeded
3 fleshy green chilies
2 garlic cloves, unpeeled
¹/₄ cup chopped onion
*¹/₄ cup trimmed and chopped fresh coriander
(cilantro)*
¹/₂ cup Fat-Free Chicken Broth (page 16)
¹/₄ tsp salt
1 small tortilla, cut into strips
2 tsp peanut oil
squeeze of lime juice

6 cod steaks, weighing about 6 ounces
salt and freshly ground black pepper
olive oil spray
1¹/₂ cups boiled rice, to serve
lime wedges, to garnish

1 Heat the oil in a heavy-based
flameproof casserole. Gently sauté the
onion and bell peppers until soft. Add
the garlic and sauté for another minute.
Stir in the tomatoes, 2 tbsp of the
parsley, the tomato paste, wine, salt,
and pepper. Bring to the boil, then
gently simmer for 10-15 minutes, until
slightly thickened.

2 Stir in the cod. Cover and simmer
for 5 minutes. Add the shrimp and
mussels. Cover and simmer for a
further 5 minutes, stirring occasionally.
Finally add the scallops. Cook for
2-3 minutes more.

3 Discard any mussels that have not
opened. Check the seasoning and
sprinkle with the remaining parsley.

4 Serve immediately,
accompanied by
saffron-flavored
rice or boiled
new potatoes.

VARIATIONS
● Use fat-free
fish broth instead
of the wine.
● Replace the cod
with monkfish,
anglerfish, or redfish.

1 To make the sauce, place the tomatillos,
bell peppers, chilies, and garlic in a
roasting pan, leaving plenty of space
between them. Roast in a preheated oven
at 450°, turning occasionally until the
skins blacken and blister. The chilies and
garlic will need about 10 minutes, the
tomatillos 10-15 minutes, and the bell
peppers 20 minutes.

2 Remove the skin from the garlic and
bell peppers, and the skin and seeds
from the chilies. Leave the tomatillos
unpeeled.

3 Place all the sauce ingredients, except
the oil and lime juice, in a food processor
or blender. Purée until smooth.

4 Heat the peanut oil in a small
saucepan until almost smoking. Add the
sauce and cook for 1-2 minutes, stirring

constantly. Add a squeeze of lime juice
and check the seasoning. Keep warm.

5 Season the cod with salt and pepper.
Spray lightly with olive oil. Place the
fish in a nonstick roasting pan under a
very hot preheated broiler for 7-9
minutes, without turning, until the flesh
is uniformly opaque.

6 Serve with the chili sauce and rice, and
garnish with lime wedges.

The green chili sauce is suitable for freezing.

NUTRITIONAL ANALYSIS

(figures are per serving including rice)

Calories = 174
Fat = 2.9g
of which saturates = 0.5g
     monounsaturates = 0.8g
     polyunsaturates = 1.0g
Protein = 29.2g
Carbohydrate = 6.3g
Dietary fiber = 2.1g
Sodium = 0.10g

Percentage of total calories from fat = 15%
of which saturates = 3%
Good source of selenium, iodine, &
B vitamins

CHAPTER FOUR

GRAINS & BEANS

*T*here is hardly a country in the world that does not have a whole-grain or bean-based dish
as part of its traditional cuisine, and with good reason. Grains and beans (also known as
legumes or pulses) are a rich source of fiber, vitamins (particularly B vitamins), minerals, and
carbohydrates. Also, being low in fat, they satisfy the appetite without piling on the pounds.
Grains and beans can be used in a variety of sweet and savory
dishes and make satisfying vegetarian entrées. Being naturally bland, they combine well
with robustly flavored ingredients such as garlic, onions, tomatoes, chilies,
soy sauce, ginger, and lime. These complement the subtle earthiness of grains and beans,
which in turn adds a mellow balance to the stronger flavors.

BREAKFAST BULGUR
WHEAT WITH DRIED FRUIT

*Cooked with grated orange zest and sweet spices, bulgur wheat makes an
energizing and virtually fat-free breakfast.*

Preparation time: 10 minutes, plus overnight soaking

Cooking time: 20 minutes

Serves 4

¹/₃ cup pitted dried apricots
¹/₃ cup pitted prunes
¹/₄ cup dried apple rings
²/₃ cup bulgur wheat
¹/₄ cup yellow or dark raisins
3 thin slivers of orange zest
crushed seeds from 3 cardamom pods
¹/₄ tsp freshly grated nutmeg

1 Place the dried apricots, prunes, and
apple rings in a bowl, cover with boiling
water, and leave to soak overnight.

2 Rinse the bulgur wheat in several
changes of water. Drain and put in a

saucepan with the raisins, orange rind,
cardamom, and nutmeg. Add enough
water to cover by the depth of your
thumbnail. Bring to the boil, then cover
and simmer over very low heat for 15
minutes until the liquid has been absorbed.

3 Divide the bulgur between individual
serving bowls, discarding the orange slivers,
and fluff with a fork. Allow to cool slightly.

4 Drain the fruit and arrange on top of
the bulgur wheat.

5 Serve with a spoonful of nonfat yogurt
and a drizzle of clear honey.

VARIATION
● Use cracked wheat or wheat
berries, soaked overnight, instead
of bulgur wheat.

COOK'S TIP
● If the cooked bulgur wheat
seems too dry, serve with
skim milk or apple juice.

BUTTERMILK
PANCAKES

Buttermilk gives these delicious light pancakes a pleasantly tangy flavor. Serve them at a lazy Sunday breakfast or brunch.

Preparation time: 10 minutes, plus 30 minutes resting

Cooking time: 25 minutes

Makes 15

1 cup self-rising flour
pinch of salt
¹/₄ tsp baking soda
1 tbsp sugar
1 extra-large egg
1¹/₄ cups buttermilk
1 tbsp sunflower or grapeseed oil
sunflower oil spray

1 Sift the flour, salt, and baking soda into a bowl. Stir in the sugar.

2 Beat the egg lightly and combine with the buttermilk.

3 Make a well in the center of the flour. Pour in half the egg-and-buttermilk mixture, and the oil. Beat with a wooden spoon, gradually drawing in the flour from around the edge. Add the remaining liquid, and whisk gently to form a smooth mixture. Pour into a measuring-jug and leave to rest for 30 minutes.

4 Lightly spray a nonstick skillet or omelet pan with oil. Heat over a medium flame. Pour in about 2 tbsp of the mixture, tilting the pan so that the batter spreads to a 5-inch circle. Cook until bubbles appear on the surface and the edges look dry. Flip over and brown the other side. Keep warm in a low oven while you cook the remaining pancakes.

5 Serve with wedges of orange and a sprinkling of sweetener or fruit purée, or a mixture of yogurt and honey.

NUTRITIONAL ANALYSIS

(figures are per serving)

Calories = 258
Fat = 1.0g
of which saturates = 0.1g
    monounsaturates = 0.0g
    polyunsaturates = 0.0g
Protein = 5. g
Carbohydrate = 59.3g
Dietary fiber = 8.5g
Sodium = 0.02g

Percentage of total calories from fat = 4%
of which saturates = 0.2%
Good source of potassium, iron, & B vitamins

NUTRITIONAL ANALYSIS

(figures are per pancake)

Calories = 56
Fat = 2.1g
of which saturates = 0.4g
    monounsaturates = 0.5g
    polyunsaturates = 1.0g

Protein = 1.9g
Carbohydrate = 7.9g
Dietary fiber = 0.3g
Sodium = 0.06g

Percentage of total calories from fat = 34%, of which saturates = 6%

SPICED PRUNE &
DATE CAKE

*This deliciously moist cake makes a substantial snack. It will
disappear in minutes, so it's worth making two!*

Preparation time: 25 minutes

Cooking time: 1 hour

Makes 14 slices

NUTRITIONAL ANALYSIS

(figures are per slice)

Calories = 142

Fat = 3.0g

of which saturates = 0.5g

    monounsaturates = 0.7g

    polyunsaturates = 1.3g

Protein = 4.4g

Carbohydrate = 26.3g

Dietary fiber = 3.1g

Sodium = 0.07g

Percentage of total calories from fat = 19%

of which saturates = 3%

Good source of iron & B vitamins

1¼ cups apple juice
½ cup chopped pitted prunes
½ cup chopped pitted dates
⅓ cup seedless raisins
1 cup all-purpose flour
1 cup whole-wheat flour
1 tsp double-acting baking powder
2 tsp ground cinnamon
½ tsp freshly grated nutmeg
¼ tsp ground cloves
¼ tsp ground allspice
¼ tsp salt
2 tbsp grapeseed or almond oil
2 eggs, lightly beaten
4 egg whites
*apple juice concentrate,
to glaze*

1 Pour 1 cup of the apple juice
into a small saucepan with the
prunes, dates, and raisins.
Bring to the boil, then cover and
simmer over gentle heat for
15 minutes. Leave to cool.

2 Combine the flours, baking
powder, cinnamon, nutmeg,
cloves, allspice, and salt.

3 Beat the oil, remaining apple
juice, and the whole eggs into
the cooled prune mixture. Stir
in the flour-and-spice mixture.

4 Beat the egg whites until stiff
but not dry. Fold about half into the
mixture to loosen it, then carefully fold
in the rest.

5 Pour into a lightly greased and floured
nonstick 8-9-inch diameter cake pan.

Leave in the pan for a few minutes
before turning out onto a wire rack
to cool.

6 Bake in a preheated oven at 325° for
1 hour until a skewer inserted in the
center comes out clean.

VARIATION

● Instead of prunes use
dried apricots.

APPLE & CINNAMON
MUFFINS

These tasty muffins are ideal for a mid-morning snack or packed lunch. Eat them on the day you make them.

Preparation time: 15 minutes

Cooking time: 15 minutes

Makes 12

²/₃ cup dried apple rings
6 tbsp sugar
1 tbsp ground cinnamon
1 cup self-rising flour
1 cup whole-wheat flour
¹/₄ tsp salt
1 cup nonfat yogurt
1 egg
2 tbsp sunflower or grapeseed oil
finely grated rind of 1 orange

1 Mince the apple rings very finely, or grind in a food processor, and set aside.

2 Mix 1 tsp of the sugar and ¹/₂ tsp of the cinnamon, and set aside for the topping.

3 Combine the remaining sugar and cinnamon with the flours and salt.

4 Whisk the yogurt, egg, oil, and orange rind in a large bowl. Add the dry ingredients, followed by the chopped apple. Stir until thoroughly mixed.

5 Lightly spray a 12-cup nonstick muffin pan with oil. Fill with the mixture, leveling with the back of a wooden spoon. Bake at 400° for 15-20 minutes, until a skewer inserted in the center comes out clean.

6 Sprinkle with the reserved cinnamon-and-sugar mixture. Spread the muffins with honey or homemade fruit jelly.

VARIATIONS
● Use dried apricots instead of apples.
● Replace the cinnamon with ¹/₂ tsp of freshly ground cardamom seeds.

NUTRITIONAL ANALYSIS
(figures are per muffin)

Calories = 152
Fat = 2.9g
of which saturates = 0.4g
monounsaturates = 0.6g
polyunsaturates = 1.5g
Protein = 3.8g
Carbohydrate = 30.2g
Dietary fiber = 2.4g
Sodium = 0.07g

Percentage of total calories from fat = 17%
of which saturates = 3%

CRANBERRY & BLUEBERRY
COFFEECAKE

This makes a sustaining virtually fat-free snack, perfect for a picnic.

Preparation time: 30 minutes, plus overnight soaking

Cooking time: 1 ¹/₂ hours

Makes 12 slices

¹/₃ cup dried cranberries
¹/₃ cup dried blueberries
³/₄ cup yellow or dark raisins
¹/₄ cup mixed candied citrus peel, minced
2 cups hot tea
1 egg, beaten
3 cups self-rising flour
4 tbsp light brown sugar

1 Place the dried fruit and mixed peel in a bowl. Add the tea and leave to soak for 8 hours or overnight.

2 Lightly spray an 8 x 5-inch nonstick loaf pan with oil. Line it with nonstick baking paper.

3 Stir the egg, flour, and sugar into the fruit mixture, mixing thoroughly. Pour into the prepared pan, pushing the mixture well into the corners and leveling the surface with a dampened metal spatula.

4 Bake in a preheated oven at 350° for 1¹/₂ hours, or until a skewer inserted in the center comes out clean.

5 Leave to cool in the pan for 10 minutes before turning out onto a wire rack and leaving to cool completely.

NUTRITIONAL ANALYSIS
(figures are per serving)

Calories = 179
Fat = 1.1g
of which saturates = 0.2g
monounsaturates = 0.3g
polyunsaturates = 0.2g
Protein = 3.9g
Carbohydrate = 41.3g
Dietary fiber = 4.9g
Sodium = 0.13g

Percentage of total calories from fat = 5%
of which saturates = 1%
Good source of calcium & iron

QUINOA SALAD
WITH GRAPES & SNOW-PEAS

This makes a light but satisfying appetizer, or you could also serve it as an accompaniment to broiled chicken or fish.

Preparation time: 20 minutes

Cooking time: 15 minutes, plus standing

Serves 4

³/₄ cup quinoa
seeds from 4 cardamom pods, crushed
2 cups water
salt
2 tsp lemon juice
1 tsp tamari (Japanese soy sauce)
2 tsp olive oil
freshly ground black pepper
²/₃ cup trimmed snow-peas
³/₄ cup halved seedless black grapes
3 tbsp snipped chives
radicchio and Bibb lettuce

NUTRITIONAL ANALYSIS

(figures are per serving)

Calories = 181
Fat = 3.9g
of which saturates = 0.5g
      monounsaturates = 1.7g
      polyunsaturates = 1.1g
Protein = 7.3g
Carbohydrate = 31.4g
Dietary fiber = 1.3g
Sodium = 0.1g

Percentage of total calories from fat = 19%
of which saturates = 2%
Good source of iron, zinc, & B vitamins

1 Dry-fry the quinoa and cardamom seeds in a small saucepan for a minute or two, until the quinoa starts to color.

2 Add the water and ¹/₂ tsp salt. Bring to the boil, then cover and simmer over very low heat for 15 minutes, until the liquid is absorbed.

3 Remove from the heat, fluff with a fork, and stir in the lemon juice, tamari, and olive oil. Transfer to a bowl and leave to cool.

4 Plunge the snow-peas into boiling water for 30 seconds, then drain. Slice diagonally into three, and stir into the quinoa.

5 Set aside a few grapes as a garnish, and add the remainder to the quinoa.

6 Stir in the chives, and salt and pepper to taste.

7 When ready to serve, arrange the lettuce leaves around the edge of a shallow serving dish or on individual plates, and pile the quinoa salad on top. Garnish with the reserved grapes and serve with crackers.

VARIATIONS

● To serve this salad as an entrée, add a tablespoon of very low-fat cottage cheese.
● Use bulgur wheat instead of quinoa.
● Use thinly sliced celery or cucumber instead of the snow-peas.

ORIENTAL
NOODLE SALAD
WITH CHICKEN

*Flavored with ginger, chili, and lime,
this substantial salad can be served as an entrée
for a light lunch or an appetizer.*

Preparation time: 30 minutes

Cooking time: 5 minutes

Serves 6

FOR THE MARINADE
*2 fresh green or red chilies, seeded and sliced into
shreds*
³/₄-inch piece fresh root ginger, minced
2 garlic cloves, crushed
3 tbsp lime juice
3 tbsp chopped fresh coriander (cilantro)
3 tbsp tamari or shoyu (Japanese soy sauce)
2 tbsp Fat-Free Chicken Broth (page 16)
¹/₂ tsp sugar
¹/₄ tsp salt
2 tsp grapeseed oil
1 tsp sesame oil

*6 ounces thin cellophane noodles
or rice noodles*
6 ounces cooked chicken breast
*3 green onions (scallions),
cut into 3-inch lengths and shredded*
¹/₄ cup thinly-sliced brown mushrooms
*¹/₃ cup cucumber, cut into
matchstick strips*
¹/₃ cup carrot, cut into matchstick strips
1 cup tender spinach, stalks removed

1 Combine all the marinade
ingredients in a bowl and leave to
stand for 15 minutes.

2 Prepare the noodles as directed on the
package. Drain and rinse in cold water.
Drain again, then cut into 6-inch
lengths. Toss with half the marinade and
set aside.

3 Tear the chicken into shreds and toss
with the remaining marinade. Add the

green onions (scallions), mushrooms,
cucumber, and carrot.

4 Stack the spinach leaves and cut
them crosswise into thin ribbons. Toss
with the noodles.

5 Arrange a mound of noodles and
spinach on individual serving dishes.
Top with the chicken mixture and serve.

NUTRITIONAL ANALYSIS

(figures are per serving)

Calories = 177
Fat = 1.5g
of which saturates = 0.3g
    monounsaturates = 0.5g
    polyunsaturates = 0.5g
Protein = 12.6g
Carbohydrate = 27.5g
Dietary fiber = 1.2g
Sodium = 0.47g

Percentage of total calories from fat = 8%,
of which saturates = 2%
Good source of iron, vitamin A, & B vitamins

VERMICELLI
WITH TOMATO & BASIL

*With a refreshing uncooked tomato sauce, this quickly made
Italian classic makes the perfect light lunch for a hot summer's day.*

Preparation time: 30 minutes, plus standing

Cooking time: 10 minutes

Serves 4

*1¼ pounds ripe plum tomatoes, peeled
1 tbsp extra virgin olive oil
1 garlic clove, crushed
salt and freshly ground black pepper
4 tbsp fresh basil
4 ounces thin pasta, such as vermicelli, taglierini,
or spaghettini
fresh basil sprigs, to garnish*

1 Slice the tomatoes, discarding the seeds and juice. Chop the flesh into ¼-inch dice and place in a bowl with the olive oil, garlic, and salt and pepper to taste.

2 Remove the basil stalks and tear the leaves into thin shreds. Mix with the tomatoes in the bowl and leave to stand for 30 minutes to allow the flavors to develop.

3 Cook the pasta in a large pan of boiling salted water until *al dente* — tender but still with some bite. Drain and transfer to a warm serving dish.

4 Check the sauce and add more seasoning if necessary, then pour over the pasta. Toss gently and serve immediately, garnished with small basil sprigs.

5 Serve the pasta with crusty bread and a simple mixed leaf salad dressed with a squeeze of lemon and plenty of chopped herbs.

COOK'S TIPS

● As with all simple dishes, success depends on top-quality ingredients. You will need perfectly ripe tomatoes with a good fruity flavor and firm flesh — they should not be at all watery. Failing this, it is better to use good quality canned tomatoes.

● The sauce needs to be well seasoned, otherwise the finished dish will be bland and tasteless.

NUTRITIONAL ANALYSIS

(figures are per serving)

Calories = 150

Fat = 3.7g

of which saturates = 0.6g

monounsaturates = 2.2g

polyunsaturates = 0.7g

Protein = 4.7g

Carbohydrate = 26.0g

Dietary fiber = 3.3g

Sodium = 0.01g

Percentage of total calories from fat = 22%

of which saturates = 4%

Good source of iron & B vitamins

FUSILLI
WITH ZUCCHINI & LEMON

*Deliciously flavored with plenty of grated lemon zest and fresh herbs,
this pasta dish is perfect for a light lunch or dinner.*

Preparation time: 25 minutes, plus draining

Cooking time: 20 minutes

Serves 4

*1 pound mixed yellow and green zucchini
salt
6 tbsp Light Vegetable Broth (page 16) or Fat-Free
Chicken Broth (page 16) for non-vegetarians
4 green onions (scallions), green parts included,
thinly sliced
1 tbsp chopped fresh rosemary
1 tbsp chopped fresh flat-leafed parsley
1 tbsp chopped fresh thyme
finely grated rind of 1 lemon
freshly ground black pepper
10 1/2 ounces pasta shapes, such as fusilli,
penne, or conchiglie (shells)
1 tbsp lemon juice
2 tbsp freshly grated Parmesan cheese*

1 Cut the zucchini into 3-inch
long matchstick strips. Put
them in a colander,
sprinkle with salt, and
leave to drain for 30
minutes. Pat dry
with paper towels.

2 Heat the broth in a large nonstick
skillet over medium heat. Add the onions,
herbs, lemon zest, and zucchini. Wet-fry
for 4-5 minutes until just tender, stirring
frequently. Season with pepper to taste.

3 Meanwhile, cook the pasta in a large
pan of boiling salted water until *al dente*
— tender but still with some bite.

4 Drain the pasta and add it
immediately to the zucchini mixture.
Stir in the lemon juice. Sprinkle with the
cheese, toss lightly, and serve.

VARIATION
● Replace the zucchini with
strips of summer squash or thin
asparagus spears.

COOK'S TIP
● Reserve some of the pasta cooking
water and add a little to the finished
dish if it seems dry.

NUTRITIONAL ANALYSIS

(figures are per serving)

Calories = 321

Fat = 4.4g

of which saturates = 1.9g

    monounsaturates = 0.8g

    polyunsaturates = 0.9g

Protein = 14.3g

Carbohydrate = 59.6g

Dietary fiber = 3.9g

Sodium = 0.09g

Percentage of total calories from fat = 12%, of which saturates = 5%

Good source of iron, zinc, selenium, vitamin A, & B vitamins

CORIANDER & CHILI
POLENTA
WITH SPICY SAUCE

*Colorful and bursting with vibrant flavors, this dish
can be served as a meat-free entrée, or in smaller quantities as an
accompaniment to broiled poultry or fish.*

Preparation time: 30 minutes

Cooking time: 45 minutes

Serves 8

1¹/₄ pounds plum tomatoes
4 fleshy green or red chilies
4 red bell peppers, halved lengthwise and seeded
2 garlic cloves, unpeeled
2 tbsp sun-dried tomato paste
1 tsp coriander (cilantro) seeds, toasted and crushed
³/₄-inch piece fresh ginger root, minced
finely grated rind of 1 lemon
¹/₂ tsp sugar
salt and freshly ground black pepper
2 cups yellow cornmeal
1 quart water
5 tbsp chopped fresh coriander (cilantro)
fresh coriander (cilantro) sprigs, to garnish

1 Place the tomatoes, chilies, bell peppers, and garlic on a cookie sheet, leaving plenty of space between them. Roast in a preheated oven at 450°, turning occasionally, until the skins blacken and blister. The chilies and garlic will need about 10 minutes, and the tomatoes and bell peppers about 20 minutes.

2 Remove the skin from the garlic and bell peppers, and the skin and seeds from the chilies. Leave the tomatoes unpeeled.

3 Mince 3 of the chilies and set aside.

4 Place the remaining chili in a food processor or liquidizer with the bell peppers, tomatoes, and garlic. Add the tomato paste, coriander (cilantro) seeds, ginger, grated lemon rind, sugar, and salt and pepper. Blend to a purée, then press through a sieve. Pour into a small saucepan and keep warm.

5 Place the cornmeal, 1 tsp of salt, and the water into a large saucepan. Bring slowly to the boil, stirring constantly with a wooden spoon or wooden stick.

6 Stir in the reserved chopped chilies and 3 tbsp of the coriander (cilantro). Cook over low heat for 15-20 minutes, stirring vigorously and frequently, until the mixture starts to pull away from the sides of the pan.

7 Pour the polenta into a 12 x 9-inch roasting pan. Spread it out evenly, smoothing the surface with dampened hands. Cut into 16 squares or diamonds. Place under the broiler to reheat if necessary.

8 Arrange 2 pieces of polenta on individual serving plates and spoon some of the sauce over it. Garnish with the remaining coriander (cilantro).

9 Serve with lightly cooked green cabbage or spinach.

VARIATION
● Instead of cutting the polenta into shapes, serve it straight from the saucepan, in the same way as creamed potato.

COOK'S TIP
● Polenta is what they call cornmeal mush in northern Italy, where it is eaten as a staple. It can be used instead of pasta, rice, or potatoes.

CHICK-PEA & MIXED-BEAN
CASSEROLE

*This hearty casserole makes a meat-free entrée,
ideal for a midweek winter dinner.*

Preparation time: 25 minutes, plus soaking

Cooking time: 1 hour

Serves 6

NUTRITIONAL ANALYSIS

(figures are per serving)

Calories = 240
Fat = 2.4g
of which saturates = 0.3g
    monounsaturates = 0.4g
    polyunsaturates = 1.1g
Protein = 17.0g
Carbohydrate = 40.5g
Dietary fiber = 14.9g
Sodium = 0.07g

Percentage of total calories from fat = 9%
of which saturates = 1%
Good source of potassium, iron, zinc,
vitamins A, E, & B vitamins

*¹/₂ cup chick-peas (garbanzo beans),
soaked overnight*
¹/₂ cup red kidney beans, soaked overnight
¹/₂ cup navy beans, soaked overnight
salt
2 cups Strong Vegetable Broth (page 16)
1 onion, minced
2 carrots, sliced
3 garlic cloves, finely chopped
¹/₄ cup green or brown lentils
14-ounce can peeled, chopped tomatoes
2 tbsp tomato paste
1 tsp dried oregano
1 tsp toasted cumin seeds
freshly ground black pepper
1¹/₂ cups green beans, sliced
*4 tbsp chopped
flat-leafed parsley*

1 Drain the chick-peas
(garbanzo beans)
and dried beans.

Place them in a
large saucepan
with fresh water to
cover. Bring to the
boil and boil rapidly for 15 minutes.
Reduce the heat to a lively simmer, and
continue to cook until tender. Add salt
during the last 10 minutes of cooking.
Drain and set aside.

2 Place 5 tbsp of the broth in a heavy-
based casserole with the onion, carrot,
and garlic. Wet-fry over a medium heat
for 4 minutes, until softened.

3 Add the lentils, tomatoes, tomato
paste, oregano, cumin, and salt and
pepper. Fry for a minute or two.

4 Add the cooked chick-peas (garbanzo
beans) and beans, and the remaining
broth. Bring to the boil, then cover and
simmer for 25 minutes.

5 Stir in the green beans and simmer for
another 10-12 minutes until tender.
Check the seasoning and stir in the
parsley before serving.

6 Serve with baked potatoes and nonfat
plain yogurt.

WILD & BASMATI RICE
PILAF
WITH DRIED CRANBERRIES

With its fruity flavors, this brightly colored pilaf makes a beautiful vegetarian main course to serve during the holidays. Served in smaller portions it makes a very low-fat accompaniment to roast turkey or chicken.

Preparation time: 25 minutes, plus cooking rice

Cooking time: 10 minutes

Serves 6

1 red onion, minced
1¹/₄ cups Light Vegetable Broth (page 16) or Fat-Free Chicken Broth (page 16) (for non-vegetarians)
3 tender celery stalks, leaves included, finely sliced
3 carrots, coarsely grated
1 fresh green chili, seeded and finely chopped
4 green onions (scallions), green parts included, thinly sliced
¹/₃ cup dried cranberries
1 tbsp olive oil
2¹/₄ cups cooked wild rice
1 cup cooked brown basmati rice
finely grated rind of 1 small orange
juice of 3 small oranges (about ¹/₂ cup)
1 tsp salt
¹/₄ tsp freshly ground black pepper

1 Place the onion and 6 tablespoons of the broth in a large nonstick skillet. Cook for 3-4 minutes, until translucent.

2 Add the celery, carrots, chilies, green onions (scallions), and cranberries. Wet-fry over medium heat for 2 minutes, until the vegetables are just tender but still crisp and brightly colored. Remove from the pan and set aside.

3 Add the oil to the pan over high heat. Stir in the rice and toss for 2 minutes to heat through. Lower the heat and stir in the grated orange rind, juice, remaining broth, and salt and pepper. Simmer for 1 minute.

4 Return the vegetables to the pan and toss with the rice to heat through before serving.

5 Serve the pilaf with Indian bread, Armenian bread, or pita pockets and a bowl of nonfat plain yogurt.

VARIATION
● Stir some puréed mango, chopped fresh coriander (cilantro), and toasted cumin seeds into the yogurt.

NUTRITIONAL ANALYSIS
(figures are per serving)

Calories = 222
Fat = 3.7g
of which saturates = 0.7g
    monounsaturates = 1.7g
    polyunsaturates = 0.9g
Protein = 4.3g
Carbohydrate = 45.9g
Dietary fiber = 5.1g
Sodium = 0.02g

Percentage of total calories from fat = 15%
of which saturates = 3%
Good source of vitamin A

TUNISIAN COUSCOUS

Serve this as a vegetarian entrée, or add 12 ounces diced extra-lean lamb.

Preparation time: 30 minutes

Cooking time: 50 minutes

Serves 6

3 cups Strong Vegetable Broth (page 16) or
Fat-Free Chicken Broth (page 16)
(for non-vegetarians)
1 onion, coarsely chopped
2 garlic cloves, crushed
1 tsp cumin seeds, toasted and crushed
1 cup canned peeled, chopped tomatoes
4 carrots, quartered
1 small celery root, cut into 1-inch pieces
4 potatoes, quartered
¹/₂ tsp hot sauce or chili powder
¹/₂ tsp salt
¹/₄ tsp freshly ground black pepper
2¹/₂ cups couscous
3 zucchini, cut
into 1-inch slices
chopped fresh coriander
(cilantro), to garnish

1 Heat 6 tbsp of the broth in a large saucepan over which a steamer will fit. Add the onion and cook over medium heat until soft.

2 Add the garlic, cumin, and tomatoes and cook for 2-3 minutes, stirring.

3 Add the carrots, celery root, potatoes, remaining broth, hot sauce or chili, and salt and pepper. Bring to the boil, cover, and simmer for 20 minutes.

4 Soak the couscous in warm water for 10 minutes. Drain thoroughly and put in a metal sieve or cheesecloth-lined steamer.

5 Add the zucchini to the vegetables, then fit the steamer over the saucepan, making sure the bottom does not touch the stew. Steam the couscous, covered, for 30 minutes, until heated through.

6 To serve, turn the couscous into a shallow serving dish and fluff with a fork. Moisten with a little broth from the vegetables. Using a slotted spoon, arrange the vegetables in the middle and garnish with coriander (cilantro). Serve the remaining vegetable broth in a pitcher.

7 Serve the couscous with pita bread and a bowl of nonfat yogurt sprinkled with ground coriander (cilantro) and a pinch of cayenne pepper.

COOK'S TIP

● Couscous consists of durum wheat grains, and looks similar to cornmeal. Ethnic stores sell it, and the special steamer in which to cook it, known as a *couscousière*.

NUTRITIONAL ANALYSIS

(figures are per vegetarian serving)

Calories − 235
Fat = 1.3g
of which saturates = 0.1g
      monounsaturates = 0.0g
      polyunsaturates − 0.4g
Protein = 7.0g
Carbohydrate = 51.8g
Dietary fiber − 3.5g
Sodium = 0.06g

Percentage of total calories from fat = 5%
of which saturates = 0.5%
Good source of iron, vitamin A, & B vitamins

CHAPTER FIVE

FRUITS & DESSERTS

*P*acked with vitamins, minerals, and fiber, and containing only minuscule
amounts of fat, fruit is a key component in a virtually fat-free diet. It supplies
the digestive system with essential bulk and fiber, and being rich in carbohydrates, helps
replace the energy normally provided by fat.
Fruit is the obvious choice for dessert, including luscious but low-fat tarts and flans and
refreshing fruit salads, yet it has a variety of other uses too. Fruit purées can
be used instead of fat to make wonderfully moist and virtually fat-free fruit bars,
and fruit soups are ideal for lazy brunches or a summer's afternoon snack.

BUTTERMILK &
RED FRUIT SOUP

*Serve this delicious fruit soup for breakfast or
as a refreshing energy-boosting snack on a hot day.*

Preparation time: 10 minutes

Cooking time: 5 minutes

Serves 4

1 tsp sunflower margarine
6 tbsp rolled (old-fashioned) oats
2 tbsp sugar
1 pound strawberries, hulled and sliced
1 cup raspberries
2¹/₂ cups buttermilk

1 Melt the margarine in a saucepan. Add
the oats and 2 tsp of the sugar. Fry over
gentle heat for a few minutes until golden.

2 Reserve one cup of the strawberries and
half a cup of the raspberries. Place the
remainder of the fruit in a blender with
the remaining sugar. Liquidize until
smooth.

3 Divide the buttermilk between 4 shallow
soup plates. Pour the berry purée into the
center and swirl slightly to mix.

4 Add the reserved whole fruit and
sprinkle with the oatmeal.

NUTRITIONAL ANALYSIS

(figures are per serving)

Calories = 218
Fat = 4.9g
of which saturates = 0.9g
    monounsaturates = 0.8g
    polyunsaturates = 0.9g
Protein = 8.9g
Carbohydrate = 36.8g
Dietary fiber = 5.3g
Sodium = 0.11g

Percentage of total calories from fat
= 20%, of which saturates = 4%
Good source of potassium, calcium,
B vitamins, & vitamin C

PEACH & MINT
SOUP

*This cooling soup would be ideal to serve as an appetizer
for a summer lunch or for a lazy weekend breakfast.
It is essential to use perfectly ripe peaches with a good flavor.*

Preparation time: 25 minutes
Serves 4

*2³/₄ pounds peaches
4 tbsp lime juice
2 tbsp orange juice
2 tbsp sugar, or to taste
4 tbsp chopped fresh mint
¹/₃ cup small-curd cottage cheese
¹/₃ cup very low-fat yogurt
4 mint sprigs, to decorate*

1 Using a small sharp knife, cut the peaches all the way round the indentation to the pit. Twist the two halves in opposite directions and ease out the pit. Remove the peel.

2 Roughly chop the flesh of all but one peach. Put the chopped flesh in a food processor or blender with 3 tbsp of the lime juice, the orange juice, sugar, and chopped mint. Liquidize until smooth. Pour into a bowl, cover, and chill.

3 Slice the remaining peach lengthwise into thin segments. Sprinkle with the remaining lime juice and set aside.

4 When ready to serve, divide the peach purée between individual serving bowls. Combine the cottage cheese and yogurt and swirl this mixture into the purée. Arrange the reserved peach slices on top and decorate with a sprig of mint.

VARIATION
● Use nectarines instead of peaches.

NUTRITIONAL ANALYSIS

(figures are per serving)

Calories = 148
Fat = 0.4g
of which saturates = 0.04g
    monounsaturates = 0.04g
    polyunsaturates = 0.02g
Protein = 5.9g
Carbohydrate = 32.0g
Dietary fiber = 6.3g
Sodium = 0.02g

Percentage of total calories from fat = 3%
of which saturates = 0.2%
Good source of potassium, B vitamins,
& vitamin C

❄ RAISIN
& APRICOT BARS

*Dried fruit purée replaces
fat in these deliciously moist
and chewy fruit bars. They
make a satisfying mid-morning
snack and are ideal for a
packed lunch box.*

Preparation time: 10 minutes,
plus soaking overnight

Cooking time: 45 minutes

Makes 16

*2 cups dried apricots, soaked overnight
1 tbsp grapeseed or sunflower oil
1 cup seedless raisins
1 cup raw oatmeal
finely grated rind of 1 lemon
$^1/_2$ tsp crushed cardamom seeds (optional)*

1 Drain the apricots, reserving the
soaking water. Put them in a small
saucepan with enough of the soaking
water to cover. Simmer for 5 minutes,
then drain off any excess liquid.
Mash with a fork or liquidize in a
blender. Beat the oil into the
mixture and leave to cool.

2 Combine the remaining
ingredients and stir them into
the apricots, mixing well.

3 Spread out the mixture in a
12 x 10-inch nonstick baking
pan, leveling the surface
with a metal spatula.

4 Bake in a preheated oven
at 400° for 40-45 minutes
until firm. Leave to cool
in the pan for a few
minutes then turn
out on to a rack to
cool completely
before cutting
into bars.

NUTRITIONAL ANALYSIS

(figures are per bar)

Calories = 88
Fat = 1.5g
of which saturates = 0.1g
      monounsaturates = 0.1g
      polyunsaturates = 0.4g

Protein = 1.8g
Carbohydrate = 18.1g
Dietary fiber = 4.2g
Sodium = 0.01g

Percentage of total calories from fat = 15%
of which saturates = 0.8%
Good source of potassium & iron

PEAR & CHERRY
CHOCOLATE BARS

Dried sour cherries give these moist, cake-like fruit bars a pleasantly tangy flavor. Serve them as a tempting snack.

Preparation time: 20 minutes

Cooking time: 25 minutes

Makes 12

1 cup less 1 tbsp all-purpose flour
1 tbsp cocoa powder
1/2 tsp ground cinnamon
1/2 tsp baking soda
1/4 tsp salt
2 tbsp sunflower margarine
2 large pears
2 tsp lemon juice
1 egg, beaten
2 tbsp sugar
1/2 cup dried sour cherries
1 tbsp pear juice concentrate

1 Sift the flour into a bowl with the cocoa powder, cinnamon, baking soda, and salt. Rub in the margarine.

2 Quarter, core, and peel the pears. Chop the flesh into tiny dice, or process briefly in a food processor, leaving the purée quite chunky.

3 Mix the pear with the lemon juice, beaten egg, and sugar.

4 Stir the dry ingredients into the pear mixture. Add the cherries, mixing well.

5 Spread the mixture in a 8 x 8 inch nonstick baking pan, smoothing the surface. Bake in a preheated oven at 350° for 20-25 minutes, until firm.

6 Allow to cool in the pan for a few minutes, then turn out onto a rack. Paint with the pear juice concentrate and leave to cool before cutting into bars.

VARIATIONS
● If you don't have any pear juice concentrate, paint the bars with a frosting made of 1 tbsp lemon juice mixed with 1/2 cup powdered (confectioner's) sugar.
● Use dried cranberries instead of the cherries.

NUTRITIONAL ANALYSIS
(figures are per bar)

Calories = 118
Fat = 2.6g
of which saturates = 0.7g
monounsaturates = 0.8g
polyunsaturates = 0.8g
Protein = 1.9g
Carbohydrate = 21.8g
Dietary fiber = 0.8g
Sodium = 0.15g

Percentage of total calories from fat = 20%
of which saturates = 5%

FRESH FIGS
WITH BERRIES & ORANGE CREAM

*A beautiful and quickly made light summer dessert served with
a low-fat, orange-flavored creamy topping.*

Preparation time: 10 minutes, plus chilling
Serves 4

*³/₄ cup very low-fat curd cheese or
sour cream substitute
2 tbsp buttermilk
1 tsp finely grated orange zest
1¹/₂ tsp sugar
4 fresh figs
1 pound fresh berries, such as raspberries,
loganberries, blueberries, mulberries, or a mixture
mint sprigs, to decorate*

1 Place the curd cheese or sour cream
substitute, buttermilk, and sugar in a
blender and liquidize for 1 minute, until
very smooth. Scrape into a bowl and stir
in the orange zest. Cover and chill.

2 Remove the stalks from the figs. Using
a small sharp knife, make a cut like a
cross in the top of each fruit, cutting
three-quarters of the way down to the
base. Hold the base with your thumb and
fingertips, and press gently so that the
fig opens out like a flower.

3 Place the figs on individual plates with
a handful of berries, and decorate with a
mint sprig. Serve with a spoonful of the
orange cream.

VARIATIONS
● Replace the figs with ripe peaches,
peeled and cut into segments.
● Mix the very low-fat curd cheese, or
low-fat sour cream substitute, and
buttermilk with sieved passion fruit
pulp instead of orange zest, or try a few
drops of rose water.

COOK'S TIP
● Use perfectly ripe, plump figs and
serve them at room temperature to
bring out their flavor.

NUTRITIONAL ANALYSIS
(figures are per serving)

Calories = 89
Fat = 0.4g
of which saturates = 0.1g
monounsaturates = 0.1g
polyunsaturates = 0.1g
Protein = 7.1g
Carbohydrate = 14.4g
Dietary fiber = 7.5g
Sodium = 0.02g

Percentage of total calories from fat = 4%
of which saturates = 1%
Good source of potassium, calcium,
B vitamins, & vitamin C

ORANGE & DATE
SALAD

*A light and simple Middle Eastern-style dessert, full of interesting flavors.
It would be perfect after a filling grain-based entrée, such as couscous.*

Preparation time: 25 minutes, plus standing time
Cooking time: 8 minutes
Serves 4

3 tbsp sugar
²/₃ cup water
7 oranges
1 tbsp shelled pistachio nuts
¹/₃ cup fresh dates, sliced lengthwise into slivers
pinch of ground cinnamon

1 Melt the sugar in a small saucepan over a gentle heat. When it turns golden, immediately remove from the heat and add the water. Return to the heat and stir until any lumps have dissolved. Allow to cool, then stir in the strained juice of one of the oranges.

2 Cover the pistachio nuts with boiling water. Leave for 5 minutes, then slip off their skins. Chop the nuts finely and set aside.

3 Using a very sharp knife, cut a horizontal slice from the top and bottom of the remaining oranges to expose the flesh. Remove the remaining peel and all the white parts by cutting downward, following the contours of the fruit.

4 Cut the flesh horizontally into thin slices, removing any seeds. Arrange attractively on individual serving dishes with the date slivers on top.

5 Spoon over some of the caramel sauce. Sprinkle with the chopped pistachio nuts and a pinch of cinnamon.

VARIATION
● Replace the dates with the seeds from 2 pomegranates.

NUTRITIONAL ANALYSIS

(figures are per serving)

Calories = 230
Fat = 2.7g
of which saturates = 0.3g
      monounsaturates − 1.1g
      polyunsaturates = 0.7g
Protein = 3.4g
Carbohydrate = 50.8g
Dietary fiber = 5.5g
Sodium = 0.04g

Percentage of total calories from fat − 11%
of which saturates = 1%
Good source of calcium, potassium, & vitamin C

STRAWBERRY
CHOCOLATE FLAN

An elegant dessert of luscious strawberries and sweetened yogurt in an almost fat-free chocolate sponge base.

Preparation time: 30 minutes

Cooking time: 25 minutes

Serves 10

sunflower oil spray
2 tsp each sugar and all-purpose flour, for sprinkling
2 eggs
2 tbsp light brown sugar
3 tbsp all-purpose flour
1 tbsp cocoa powder
1 cup nonfat plain yogurt
1 tsp sugar
1 cup strawberries, halved
mint sprig, to decorate

1 Lightly spray with oil a 9-inch raised-base pie pan. Sprinkle with sugar, tilting to coat evenly. Sprinkle with flour, tapping the pan to remove any excess.

2 Using a hand-held electric beater, whisk the eggs and sugar in a deep bowl until creamy and thick. The mixture should double in volume and leave a trail which you can still see for 5 seconds after the whisk has been removed.

3 Sift the flour and cocoa over the surface. Lightly fold in with a metal spoon.

4 Pour the mixture into the prepared pan and level the surface. Place on a cookie sheet and bake in a preheated oven at 350° for 20-25 minutes, until springy to touch. Turn out on to a wire rack and leave to cool.

5 Mix the yogurt and sugar together, then spread over the base. Arrange the strawberries on top and decorate with a sprig of mint.

The flan base is suitable for freezing.

NUTRITIONAL ANALYSIS

(figures are per serving)

Calories = 93
Fat = 1.9g
of which saturates = 0.6g
      monounsaturates = 0.7g
      polyunsaturates = 0.2g
Protein = 4.4g
Carbohydrate = 15.9g
Dietary fiber = 0.7g
Sodium = 0.04g

Percentage of total calories from fat = 18%
of which saturates = 6%
Good source of vitamin C

RHUBARB, STRAWBERRY, & ANISE

PHYLLO PIE

Rhubarb and strawberries flavored with anise are a surprisingly good combination. The pastry case made of phyllo dough keeps the fat content down.

Preparation time: 35 minutes
Cooking time: 25 minutes
Serves 8

1 pound trimmed young rhubarb
1¼ pounds strawberries
⅔ cup sugar
1½ tbsp cornstarch
finely grated rind of 2 oranges
seeds from 6 star anise pods, crushed
6 sheets phyllo dough, measuring
10 inches square, defrosted
2 tsp grapeseed oil
1 tbsp powdered (confectioner's) sugar
1 tsp orange flower water

1 Slice the rhubarb diagonally into 1½-inch lengths. Cut the strawberries in half lengthwise.

2 Combine the sugar and cornstarch in a shallow ovenproof dish. Add the rhubarb and strawberries, and sprinkle with the grated orange rind and half the star anise seeds, turning to coat. Leave to stand, turning occasionally while you prepare the pastry case.

3 Cover the phyllo sheets with a clean, damp kitchen towel. Taking one sheet at a time, lightly dab with oil on one side only. Place in a lightly greased 9-inch diameter 1½-inch deep loose-bottomed pie pan. Gently press the dough into the edge of the pan. Cover with the remaining dough, rotating each sheet so the corners are offset to resemble the petals of a flower.

4 Mix the powdered (confectioner's) sugar and orange flower water to a paste and use to paint the dough "petals."

5 Bake the rhubarb-and-strawberry mixture and the pastry case separately in a preheated oven at 375°. Bake the pastry for 10-15 minutes until golden and crisp, taking care that the edges do not burn. Bake the filling for 15-20 minutes, until the rhubarb is only just tender and still holds its shape.

6 Carefully ease the pastry out of the pan and place on a serving platter. Using a perforated cooking spoon, fill the case with the strawberries and rhubarb.

7 Pour the juice into a small saucepan. Bring to the boil and cook until it has a syrupy consistency. Spoon the syrup over the fruits. Sprinkle with the reserved star anise seeds. Serve warm.

COOK'S TIP
● Remove the filling from the oven while the rhubarb is still firm. It quickly loses its shape if overcooked.

NUTRITIONAL ANALYSIS

(figures are per serving)

Calories = 142
Fat = 1.11g
of which saturates = 0.1g
      monounsaturates = 0.1g
      polyunsaturates = 0.5g
Protein = 1.9g
Carbohydrate = 33.4g
Dietary fiber = 2.7g
Sodium = 0.01g

Percentage of total calories from fat = 7%,
of which saturates = 0.5%
Good source of potassiun & vitamin C

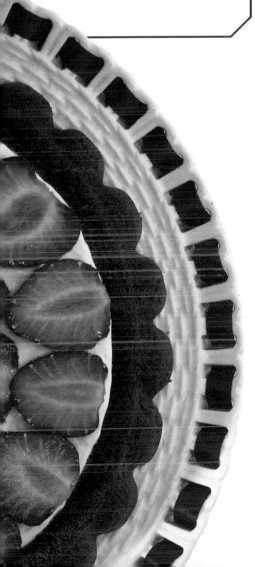

TROPICAL TAPIOCA

Preparation time: 15 minutes

Cooking time: 15 minutes

Serves 6

³/₄-inch piece fresh ginger root, minced
4 tbsp pearl tapioca
2¹/₂ cups skim milk
8 passion fruits (granadillas)
2 tbsp sugar
3 tbsp lime juice
lime twists, to decorate

1 Place the ginger, pearl tapioca, and milk in a saucepan. Bring to the boil, stirring, then simmer, continuing to stir, for 15 minutes, until thickened. Leave to cool.

2 Scoop out the pulp from the passion fruits (granadillas), including the seeds. Mix with the sugar and lime juice.

3 Stir the passion fruit (granadilla) mixture into the tapioca. Pour into a serving bowl or sundae glasses. Add extra sugar or lime juice to taste. Cover and chill.

4 Decorate with twists of lime and serve.

NUTRITIONAL ANALYSIS

(figures are per serving)

Calories = 122
Fat = 0.4g
of which saturates = 0.2g
      monounsaturates = 0.1g
      polyunsaturates = 0.1g
Protein = 4.2g
Carbohydrate = 27.4g
Dietary fiber = 0.0g
Sodium = 0.06g

Percentage of total calories from fat = 3%
of which saturates = 1%
Good source of iron & B vitamins

BAKED BANANAS WITH LIME CREAM

Hot, fragrant bananas with a lime-flavored creamy topping are a heavenly combination in this easy dessert.

Preparation time: 20 minutes

Cooking time: 20 minutes

Serves 4

3 tbsp clear honey
juice of 2 limes
4 bananas
4 tbsp very low-fat curd cheese or
very low-fat small-curd cottage cheese
1 tbsp buttermilk
1 tbsp plain nonfat yogurt
¹/₂ tbsp sugar, or to taste

1 Melt the honey in a small saucepan, then mix with all but 1 tbsp of the lime juice.

2 Peel the bananas and halve lengthwise. Place in a shallow ovenproof dish into which they fit snugly. Spoon the honey mixture over them. Bake in a preheated oven at 425° for 10-15 minutes, until soft and slightly bubbling.

3 Meanwhile, beat the curd cheese or small-curd cottage cheese, buttermilk, yogurt, and sugar until smooth. Stir in the remaining lime juice.

4 Arrange the bananas on individual plates and pour the juices over them. Serve at once with a spoonful of lime cream.

VARIATION

● Flavor the honey with minced stem ginger, or the seeds from 8 cardamom pods.

NUTRITIONAL ANALYSIS

(figures are per serving)

Calories = 148
Fat = 0.4g
of which saturates = 0.1g
      monounsaturates = 0.0g
      polyunsaturates = 0.1g

Protein = 3.6g
Carbohydrate = 34.8g
Dietary fiber = 3.1g
Sodium = 0.01g

Percentage of total calories from fat = 2%, of which saturates = 0.7%
Good source of potassium

BROILED PEPPERED
PINEAPPLE

This impressive dessert requires a very ripe, sweet pineapple for success.

Preparation time: 30 minutes

Cooking time: 15 minutes

Serves 4

1 tbsp shelled pistachio nuts
6 tbsp clear honey
12 black or green peppercorns, crushed
juice of 1 orange
2 tbsp lime juice
2 small pieces preserved ginger, minced
1 small ripe pineapple
4 tsp sugar

1 Cover the pistachio nuts with boiling water and leave to stand for 5 minutes. Slip off the skins, chop the nuts finely, and set aside.

2 Place the honey, peppercorns, grated orange rind and juice, lime juice, and ginger in a small saucepan. Bring to the boil, then simmer for 5 minutes until reduced by half.

3 Peel and core the pineapple, and cut into about 8 ½-inch thick slices. Cut in half and arrange in a single layer in a nonstick ovenproof dish. Sprinkle with the sugar. Place under a preheated very hot broiler for 5-8 minutes, turning once, until browned and bubbling. Pour the sauce over the slices and broil for 1 minute more.

4 Arrange on individual plates and spoon the juices over the fruits. Sprinkle with the pistachio nuts and serve hot.

VARIATION
● Peppercorns add a subtle warm flavor which contrasts well with the pineapple, but you can omit them if you wish.

NUTRITIONAL ANALYSIS
(figures are per serving)

Calories = 183
Fat = 2.7g
of which saturates = 0.3g
monounsaturates = 1.3g
polyunsaturates = 0.9g
Protein = 1.7g
Carbohydrate = 40.7g
Dietary fiber = 2.1g
Sodium = 0.03g

Percentage of total calories from fat = 13%,
of which saturates = 2%
Good source of potassium & vitamin C

PLUM
YOGURT ICE

*Low-fat plain yogurt gives this mouthwatering
ice dessert a wonderfully creamy taste.*

Preparation time: 20 minutes, plus cooling, beating, and freezing

Cooking time: 20 minutes

Serves 8

*1¼ pounds red plums
2½ cups water
1 cup sugar
finely grated rind of 1 orange
2 tsp lemon juice
2 tbsp brandy or dessert wine (optional)
1 cup low-fat plain yogurt
3 tbsp seedless raisins*

1 Cut the plums round the indentation through to the pit. Twist the 2 halves sharply in opposite directions to loosen the pit, then scoop it out with a knife. Cut the flesh lengthwise into thin segments and place in a bowl.

2 Place the water, sugar, and grated orange rind in a saucepan. Heat gently until the sugar has dissolved. Raise the heat and boil for 10 minutes, until syrupy.

3 Immediately pour the syrup over the plums. Leave to cool at room temperature.

4 Strain the syrup and set aside.

5 Finely chop about a quarter of the plums. Liquidize the remainder in a food processor or blender with the lemon juice. Transfer to a large bowl and add the chopped plums. Stir in the brandy or dessert wine, if using, then fold in the yogurt and 1 cup of the reserved syrup.

6 Freeze in an ice-cream maker, following the manufacturer's instructions, or pour into a shallow freezerproof container. Cover the surface with plastic wrap. Freeze for about 2 hours, until beginning to harden round the edges.

7 Transfer to a mixing bowl and whisk until smooth. Freeze again. Repeat the process twice more if you have time, then freeze until completely firm.

8 To make the sauce, place the remaining syrup in a saucepan with the raisins. Bring to the boil, then boil rapidly for 3 minutes, until reduced slightly. Remove from the heat and leave to cool.

NUTRITIONAL ANALYSIS

(figures are per serving)

Calories = 172
Fat = 2.2g
of which saturates = 1.4g
     monounsaturates = 0.5g
     polyunsaturates = 0.1g
Protein = 1.7g
Carbohydrate = 36.5g
Dietary fiber = 1.7g
Sodium = 0.05g

Percentage of total calories from fat = 12%
of which saturates = 7%